ALL ABOUT
Yvie
INTO THE ODDITY

YVIE ODDLY
with MICHAEL BACH

GREENLEAF
BOOK GROUP PRESS

This book is a memoir reflecting the authors' present recollections of experiences over time. Its story and its words are the authors' alone. Some details and characteristics may be changed, some events may be compressed, and some dialogue may be recreated. Some names and identifying characteristics of persons referenced in this book, as well as identifying places, have been changed to protect the privacy of the individuals and their families.

Published by Greenleaf Book Group Press
Austin, Texas
www.gbgpress.com

Distributed by Greenleaf Book Group

For ordering information or special discounts for bulk purchases, please contact Greenleaf Book Group at PO Box 91869, Austin, TX 78709, 512.891.6100.

Design and composition by Greenleaf Book Group
Cover design by Greenleaf Book Group

Publisher's Cataloging-in-Publication data is available.

Print ISBN: 979-8-88645-199-3

eBook ISBN: 979-8-88645-200-6

To offset the number of trees consumed in the printing of our books, Greenleaf donates a portion of the proceeds from each printing to the Arbor Day Foundation. Greenleaf Book Group has replaced over 50,000 trees since 2007.

Printed in the United States of America on acid-free paper

24 25 26 27 28 29 30 31   11 10 9 8 7 6 5 4 3 2

First Edition

I dedicate this book to my cats, for whom I'm eternally grateful. I know your affection might not come easily and is often misunderstood, but this is why mommy works so damn hard! It's all worth it for the sweet reward of hearing your furry li'l purries. I promise that someday you will have all the finest things this mortal life has to offer such divine beings.

Also, you have permission to eat me when I die.

—Yvie

CONTENTS

WHAT DREAMS MAY COME

It's a little strange writing a book about yourself. Like, how fragile does a person's ego have to be to publish a cry for validation? It's even more strange considering that most memoirs are written *after* the peak of someone's career. Not at the beginning. You read that right, so let's be clear. No matter where you're picking up in my story, it's just getting started.

A few years ago, I decided I wanted to put out a book because there were some pretty radical things that happened in my life, and I felt those stories would best be told in print. But I'm not entirely a writer. Sure, I may have published a couple of literary magazines in high school, but nowadays my art is mostly visual and performance. I think in the visual. When I come up with my outfits, I often see them in my dreams, or in the natural world around me. Not in concrete designs necessarily, but in the abstract. Like for my look for the "Veiled It" runway on *RuPaul's Drag Race All Stars, All Winners*—I had been plagued by a series of dreams about floating triangles, colorful sparkling beads, and a woman wrapped in a blanket wandering through the desert. None of these dreams really meant anything on their own, but I followed them into the waking hours of creativity regardless. For weeks I would wake up in the middle of the night and be driven by the urge to sew, stone, create. Did I feel insane? Sure. But the result was an iconic look that I got to bring to the runway. That's how I create my art—whether it be my drag, my visual art, or my music.

Writing is different because I speak like I think—stream of consciousness. My brain is always two steps ahead of my mouth, and what comes out is sometimes not as coherent as I want it to be. So it takes a lot of time for me to form my thoughts into the words that accurately convey them. Needless to say, the idea of writing a book was and is daunting. It's one thing to write a few hundred words of rap for my single "Vibe" (available now on iTunes), but it's another thing entirely to figure out a fifty-thousand-word book!

So, when I met Michael—who you'll meet in the next chapter—it was one of those moments where the universe puts something or someone in front of you and you think, "Shit, that was some great timing." Which brings us to this moment.

This book is an exploration of my life up until a point. It's not the final chapter of my life, but it gets us to the middle-ish. It's been a wild fucking ride and I think it's a story worth telling. It covers my childhood, and all the wonderful and chaotic shit that shaped my worldview. It covers my coming out and the exploration of my sexuality and gender. And it covers my drag. Not just *Drag Race*, but we get into my drag BR and AR: Before RuPaul and After RuPaul. There is no doubt that *RuPaul's Drag Race* obviously has been a big part of my career. If I hadn't been on *Drag Race*, I probably wouldn't be in a position to publish a book, because not enough people would give a shit. But my drag has a story before I walked into the Werk Room, and it's had a helluva lot of story since then.

I'm going to talk about my fans, and what my relationship has been like with the fandom in general because y'all know that shit has been spicy. I wanted to include something about my interactions with the fans because, as I have learned, Twitter (or whatever the fuck it's called today) is not the best medium to express a complex thought. It will be little surprise that I have some strong feelings about how some fans treat celebrities. How in some facet there's this common feeling of ownership over public figures, which I think is bullshit. It's this mindset and certain behaviors it accompanies that really piss me off, and as you likely already know, I'm not one to keep that shit to myself. That being said, I want to clear the air. I love my fans. Immensely. Thank you for seeing something special in me and, by extension, yourself.

I'd also like to shed some perspective on my gender identity, and in quite a bit of detail. People are always asking me, "What are your pronouns?" As if sharing whether I use he/him, she/her, they/them, or some other pronoun could possibly explain how I see my gender in every given moment. I'm going to use this word, and people may not like it, but I'm going to use this word that I *transitioned* into the drag queen that I am now. I use transitioning because it is a transition. As much as there is a facet of our movement that's like, 'Drag queens are not Trans women, and it's not the same thing.' For me, it actually is a part of how I express my innate Transness. I will never go so far as to try and actually appropriate some lived experience and say I'm a Trans woman too. But I've always felt Trans before I knew what that word was, before I knew what it meant. And after I discovered what it meant, it didn't feel like me because there were only specific ways to be Trans. So, it's only in the last few years that I've been like, "Oh, wait, no, no, no, I am Trans. I'm just too unmotivated to do much of anything about my gender expression outside of drag." This is all to say that in this book I will be using they/them pronouns because of how they encompass all the facets of my identity that different people in my life refer to.

The last major piece of this book is about the person I share my life with: Doug, or Mr. Oddly, as Michael calls him. And he is that, in that we got married in the summer of 2023, although he didn't change his last name to Oddly because that would be fucking weird. My relationship with Doug is far from typical, as you can imagine. Being in a relationship with a drag queen can be challenging. We mostly work at night and crave the spotlight. Drag queens are fucking attention whores. We don't become drag queens because we wish we could be at home knitting. It takes a special person to be able to balance us out—be the ying to our yang or whatever. But then add to that the shitshow that can be the life of a successful Ru girl, and it can be pandemonium. And it has been, but in all the best kinds of ways.

Doug and I met at the perfect moment: on Grindr (because where the fuck else do people meet nowadays) on January 23, 2019—the day before the cast announcement of season 11 of *RuPaul's Drag Race*. So, Doug didn't know me before *Drag Race*, but he also didn't know me after it. We were getting to know each other in the two months between the cast announcement and the show airing, and then in the three months of the show airing. What a fucking trip that was. He got to see me in some of my worst moments on television, and a lot of times he would look at me and say, "What the fuck was that about?" But it was through that experience that we grew close, and figured out how to be in a relationship, when he was home being a lawyer and I was flipping my ass around the world. And of course there was some drama, which you're going to hear all about.

Doug is my rock. He's my person. He's my best friend. He's the only person I've ever known who can give me the love I need, exactly when I need it, but also not put up with my bullshit when I'm acting like a petulant child. He also gives me the space to create and be Yvie, while still being there as my biggest supporter.

This book isn't a tell-all. I didn't want to have my first book be some "behind the scenes of *RuPaul's Drag Race*" bullshit. Is there tea—aka talk or gossip—about what happens when the cameras aren't rolling? Of course. Is that interesting enough to write a whole book about? Not really. Definitely not to me. If you want to know the behind-the-scenes dirt, there are enough queens online who will spill it. Or just go on Reddit, because apparently someone there has the inside scoop on every footstep.

That's not to say this book is fluffy bullshit, either. Anyone who knows me knows that's not my style. When I read this book—and I've read it numerous times—the word that comes to mind is "raw." The interview process was tough at times. Michael and I spent more than thirty hours talking (including one time when I was in the bathtub. Thanks, Zoom), digging into parts of my life that I hadn't thought about in a long time. Like my first childhood memory. Or the heaps of trauma I've experienced. I cried a lot. Secretly, I think it was Michael's goal to get me to cry every time we spoke. He succeeded. But to make this book successful—to tell the story I feel I owe to the fans—I needed to be willing to dig deep and not just let you see the Yvie that I want people to see. I wanted you to see the real me. The truthful me.

You're going to hear from a cast of characters in my life as well, so it's not just me. There's my parents, Jessyca and Sheps, who shared things I didn't even know. My bestie Teena, who was right there with me through the *RPDR* experience. Doug, of course. And even my old teacher Deb Rosenbaum from Denver School of the Arts had something to say. And this book wouldn't be complete without hearing from a bunch of other Ru girls who I've had the opportunity to work with, share with, yell at, and now call sisters. I was a bit worried about what they would say, but my story isn't complete without hearing from them.

I hope you enjoy the book. I really do. Believe it or not, my goal is always to ensure my fans are enjoying the art that I put out in the world. But if you don't, you're welcome to kindly fuck yourself.

Love ya, bitches.

—Yvie

@oddlyyvie

THE DREAM CHASERS

Who is Yvie Oddly? I mean, I know who Yvie Oddly is, but who are they *really*? What makes them tick? Where do they get their ideas from? What was *Drag Race* really like for them? And most important, who are they when the cameras aren't rolling?

I remember the moment when they walked into the Werk Room on season 11 of *RuPaul's Drag Race*, and my immediate thought was, "What in the name of the sweet baby Jesus is this queen wearing?" But after the shock wore off, my next thought was, "This queen has something!" I didn't know what Yvie had but it was that *je ne sais quoi*, which is French . . . for something. As Kandy Muse screamed on her season, it was "star quality." Yvie has star quality.

Now, you might be thinking, "I just bought Yvie Oddly's biography. Who the fuck is this person writing, because it's clearly not

Yvie Oddly, or Yvie has finally slipped into the abyss of madness, and her newest personality sounds like an accountant." No, you're right, this isn't Yvie writing. Although they are close to that madness thing.

My name is Michael Bach. Who I am isn't really relevant, but since you asked, I'll share. First, I'm an author. I've written two best-selling and award-winning books, along with countless articles in a bunch of publications you've likely heard of. I'm not Yvie-famous but some people know my name, and not just my parents.

I'm also a recovered actor who performed in drag a few times. My last time in drag was a 2004–2005 tour of a live-sung drag sister act called the *Daisy and Wilma Show*. I played Daisy Chain and my friend Christian played my sister Wilma Holehurt. We toured Canada and the United States singing in countless LGBTQIA+ bars and clubs from sea to shining sea. I was gorgeous and skinny . . . largely because we were barely making ends meet and I was surviving on a diet of gin and low-sodium air. But I hung up the heels after that to pursue other opportunities that didn't involve shaving my chest. Not as a requirement anyway. I now make my living working in the field of inclusion, diversity, equity, and accessibility.

Lastly, I'm a *Drag Race* superfan (self-proclaimed because the paperwork to make it official was brutal!). I started watching *RuPaul's Drag Race* on February 2, 2009—the day the show first aired. I remember the first moment of the first episode, at two minutes and twenty-three seconds, when Shannel walked into the Werk Room with her eyebrows as high as the sky and her ass exposed for all the world to see. I was hooked. Are you kidding?

There were drag queens on television and we weren't the butt of the joke. We got to see positive queer representation on the screen. This was a show that celebrated drag. Yes, the set looked like they filmed in RuPaul's parents' garage, and the lighting made everyone look like they were using a really shitty Instagram filter, but still . . . it was magical. It was forty-four minutes and nineteen seconds of absolute joy, and I loved every single queen that walked into the Werk Room: Akashia, BeBe Zahara Benet, Jade Sotomayor, Nina Flowers, Ongina, Rebecca Glasscock, Shannel, Tammie Brown, and Victoria "Porkchop" Parker. Every one of them was my hero.

Since then, I have watched every single episode of every single season, from every single country. Some call it an addiction. I like to think of it as a calling. During the COVID-19 pandemic, not a week went by without some *Drag Race*, and at times there were two and three shows on the go at the same time. I hardly had time for my job. And my husband . . . I'm sure he's here somewhere.

Truthfully, I was envious when the show came on. Had the show aired a few years earlier, I would have been sending in my audition tape to be America's next drag superstar. But alas, as Ru would say, it was not my time.

In 2020, when everyone in the world was locked away in their homes, I had an idea. I am an author. I can write. What if I was to write about some of the queens from *Drag Race*? So, I started reaching out to a select few of my favorites whom I wanted to know more about. And the first one to bite was none other than Yvie Oddly, winner of season 11, and one of the most delightful, talented, complex, and intelligent queens out there. Yvie is the perfect example of someone I wanted to know more about.

Yvie and I set out on a journey to craft a book that tells their story. Over several months, I had the pleasure of having one-on-one time with Yvie; their mother Jessyca; their father Sheps; their best friend Teena; one of their teachers, Deb; their boyfriend (now husband) Doug; and many of their drag family, including Asia O'Hara, Brooke Lynn Hytes, Naomi Smalls, Nina Flowers, Silky Nutmeg Ganache, and Venus D-Lite. The words in this book come directly from all of them. I am simply the humble narrator sewing the stories together like a tapestry.

This book is all about Yvie. From their birth, to coming out, to their evolution as a drag artist, to their rise to global superstardom. This book is not a tell-all, but that doesn't mean there isn't an ample serving of tea. If there's one thing Yvie didn't do during our hours and hours of conversations, it is hold back. They were honest and open. They tapped into a lot of their past to share their truth.

They wanted to lay bare their soul for this book to show the fandom who they really are. At times the process was difficult, when we were digging into some very painful memories. At times there was anger, as they shared their frustration with certain people and experiences. At times there was joy and laughter—that laugh the world has come to adore (unless you're in a movie theater with them, and then the laugh is a liability).

I wanted this book to be a love letter to the fandom. I have gotten to do something that very few people have—I have had the chance to get to know Yvie Oddly on a very deep level. I've come to see them for who they are—brilliantly talented, incredibly complex, deeply intelligent, somewhat insecure, angry, kind, gentle, and beautiful. I hope that as you read these pages you will see what I see.

A note about pronouns: Yvie's gender can best be described as fluid. Some people refer to them as "he," and some as "she," but truth be told, Yvie doesn't actually care. You can use any pronoun with Yvie and they're happy, as long as it's respectful. For the purposes of this book, we'll be using "they" for the most part, because it's just easier than anything (although you will see a few "he's" and "she's" on occasion). For some, that will be a new experience—reading text that uses "they" and "them" in the singular. You'll see sentences like, "They told a story . . ." This is done deliberately to respect who Yvie is and how they identify.

A warning about language: The quotes in this book include some language that some may find difficult. However, in order to ensure this book is authentic, I haven't changed the language of quotes from interview subjects to make it more palatable. Just know that there are some things that might be difficult for some to read. You've been warned.

Now, let the games begin.

—Michael

@TheMichaelBach

YVIE'S TOP 5 FAVORITE WORDS

1. Lugubrious: "mornful, dismal, or gloomy, especially in an affected, exaggerated, or unrelieved manner" (And it sounds like lube.)

2. Petrichor: "the pleasant, earthy smell after rain" (Unless you're in New York and then all you smell is urine.)

3. Clinomania: "excessive desire to stay in bed" (Everyday. All day.)

4. Sozzled: "hammered, wrecked, drunk." (Tuesday.)

5. Winklepicker: "a shoe or boot that features a sharp-pointed toe" (Makes the list not because of the meaning, but because it sounds dirty.)

CHAPTER 1

IN THE BEGINNING, THERE WAS JOVAN

Once upon a time there was a nerdy (self-described, and in all the best ways) little girl named Jessyca. She loved animals and wanted to be a veterinarian but couldn't imagine having to put an animal down, so that dream was a no-go. It's a harsh world. But that's not important. This isn't Jessyca's story, but she's pretty integral to the plot.

One day, in junior high, Jessyca met Khalil (who in 1997 changed his name to Sheps. That's not relevant to the story and it doesn't matter why. It's just here so it doesn't confuse you. Khalil and Sheps are the same person).

In the summer between sixth and seventh grades, Sheps met a girl at the local YMCA, and as many eleven-year-olds do, he crushed on her hard. So, when he returned to school and ran into that same girl in the hall, he naturally gave her his telephone number. That girl turned out to be Jessyca's sister, who in turn gave Sheps's number to Jessyca. While not the outcome Sheps had hoped for, he and Jessyca became good friends. They talked every day, walked to school, and went to parties together. But they were just friends, or at least that was what Sheps thought.

According to Jessyca, "He was my best friend through high school. But I was madly in love with him, obviously. I mean, he was gorgeous. I kind of followed him around like a puppy dog. And he was a ladies' man. There was always some girl, and I used to tease him quite a bit, like, 'Yeah you might be handsome, but you're not all that. Because you got this thing where you have to have all these women. And it's not attractive. Settle down with one girl.' So, there was that dynamic in our relationship. But he was still my best friend . . . for a while."

How Sheps was, and is, may be connected to his upbringing, as most of our behavior is. Sheps's father was Lauren Watson, who is a legend in Denver's African American community. Sheps explains, "I was born and raised in Denver. I've only left the state once, that was for college. I went to Howard University. My parents were both revolutionaries. My dad, along with my mother, started the Black Panthers in Denver. We couldn't walk a block in a crowded area without my dad being stopped two hundred times. So, instead of breakfast at a restaurant taking forty-five minutes, it would take three hours and forty-five minutes. But on the flip side, we also grew up with our phones being tapped and being followed by police and all that kind of wonderful J. Edgar Hoover stuff." While the fact that Sheps's parents were the founders of the Denver chapter of the Black Panthers may seem immaterial to Yvie's story, it's an important little detail as to who Sheps was and is, and the father he became.

In high school, Sheps found himself in conflict with his teachers because their perspective on world events varied from that of his parents. As Sheps explains, "I had a lot of historical background. I ended up being a history major, knowing that the stuff I was being taught was not the stuff that, first of all, was important to me, and second of all, a lot of it was just brushed over." The conflict with his teachers led Sheps to become somewhat of a rebel. And who doesn't love a bad boy? Put together his exceptional looks with his James Dean *Rebel Without a Cause* attitude and it's an instruction manual on how to get laid.

Jessyca wasn't exactly a wallflower. She got pregnant in her junior year of college. As she explains, "I didn't know who the father was. Because I had an affair with Khalil. But I was in a relationship with the man that was to be the love of my life—Ronnie. And Jason was the other guy that I was practically living with."

One fateful afternoon, August 22, 1993, Jovan Jordan Bridges, or Jo, as his mama calls him, came into the world. "The most striking thing about Jo when he was born was when they put him on my chest, the first thing he did was he lifted his head. I was amazed. I was like, 'You are not the little baby I thought you were going to be.' I expected this helpless, poor little thing. He lifted his head, and he looked at me with these big brown eyes, and I was just awestruck. Not only that he was doing that, but that I was completely overwhelmed with love for him.

"I always thought I was going to have a girl. When I was pregnant with him, I was determined. 'Yeah! This is definitely a girl. I know it in my heart of hearts.' I painted my room pink, I had little frilly curtains, because that was going to be me and my baby girl's room."

Now back to who the father is. During her pregnancy, and up until the day of Jovan's birth, Jessyca was confident that the father was Jason, whom she was living with. She wasn't certain but her gut instinct was that it was Jason's baby. But the truth became apparent when the doctors handed Jessyca her new baby boy. "I looked at him and I knew immediately whose child he was. He looked just like Khalil when he was a baby. He had Khalil's nose. I didn't say a word to Jason because he kept looking Jo over, saying, 'Oh, he has my feet, my toes.' I was like, 'He does not. No, he does not!' So, I immediately called Khalil and said, 'This is your son.'

"Khalil came to the hospital, and I think he was in shock, but he was just being there more as a friend. In his mind he wasn't accepting that this was his child. He kind of laughed about it. He was like, 'Well, *maybe* he is. I can't believe this is happening.' But he didn't take it very seriously until time had passed, and I kept pushing, saying, okay, this really is your son. I finally told Jason, 'This is not your son. This is Khalil's son.' Khalil refused to accept it and Jason was the complete opposite. He said, 'Well, I want to take a paternity test and prove that he's my son.' Because he'd fallen in love with the baby before the baby was born. In fact, his name Jovan comes from Jason. Jason's the one who came up with that name."

Even without the paternity test, Jessyca's belief that baby Jo was Sheps's had a chain reaction. Jason left. Ronnie left. And much to Jessyca's objections, Sheps left to go to Howard University in Washington, DC. Sheps had always planned to go to Howard. Because of his parents' influence, he wanted to study history at one of the country's most prestigious Historically Black Colleges and Universities. He didn't run *away* from Jessyca and baby Jo, but he certainly didn't run *to* them either.

So, here was Jessyca, barely twenty-one years old, a single mother with a newborn baby, trying to get a college education, in medicine, no less. But Jessyca wasn't alone. She lived with her parents, who helped immensely. As she explains, "My dad—because I had given birth to Jo—went to school for me for a week and took notes. Now, my dad is a business guy. He's not at all in medicine, so I really applaud him for doing that. He did a great job. And I would study the notes when he would bring them home."

Raising Jo became a family affair. In addition to her parents, there were many others who helped out. As Jessyca explains, "One of dad's ex-girlfriends was babysitting him for a little while, because he was too young to go to day care, so she babysat him for probably the first couple of months or so. Ultimately, I put him in a Montessori school when he was about four months old, when they would finally accept him."

Eventually, Sheps agreed to do a paternity test and discovered that Jovan was, in fact, his son. And to his credit, Sheps stepped up. As he explains, "I wrote out a bunch of checks, because I had always had a job. I wrote out a year's worth of checks and my mom would give her a check every month. And every time I came home from school, I would go spend time with them and pick them up, and we'd hang out and stuff like that. So, there was never one of those times—well, there was never *voluntarily* a time—where I didn't spend time with him."

Eventually, Sheps came home from Howard and wanted to be part of Jo's life, but there was conflict with Jessyca, who didn't like how Sheps was parenting Jovan. She felt he wasn't putting enough into the relationship.

Sheps has a different perspective: "She thought I was a wonderful father to my daughter Zakayla. She had different criteria when it came to me raising and being a part of my son's life. There was some deeper stuff going on. I think she expected me to not go to school out of state. She expected us to be in a relationship. But we had never been in a relationship, so it just didn't seem like the direction to go."

By the time Sheps came back from Howard, Jessyca had met and moved in with the man she would marry and who would become Jovan's stepfather—Don. Jovan was just nine months old when she met Don—while she was still living at home with her parents—but he stepped in and stepped up by helping to raise little baby Jo. Yet, Jovan's relationship with Don was, to put it mildly, complicated, which began at a very early age. As Jessyca tells it, "When I did finally move into my own place, I didn't have a bed for Jo, so he slept in my bed. Don did not like that! Don went and bought him this little car bed and he said, 'Jo is going to sleep in his own bed, and we're going to make it fun, and try to get him to sleep in that bed.' So, Jo and Don immediately clashed from the very beginning, because Don was pushing him out of his mama's bed."

By all accounts, Jovan was a smart, happy baby, and he was very close to his mother. "I would listen to Sade all the time and he would dance," Jessyca recalls. "He knew all the lyrics when he was itty-bitty. It was so cute! I have this one memory of him sitting in his car seat, and 'Like a Tattoo' was playing on the radio. Jo was barely talking but he would sing, 'Tattoooo.' He was just so adorable and incredibly smart."

Jessyca saw Jovan's intellectual potential very early on and she focused on developing that. Rather than just reading him stories, she would read books on history and science to help expand his education. Deb Rosenbaum, Yvie's teacher from Denver School of the Arts (DSA), agrees that Yvie possessed a significant level of intelligence at an early age: "I would start talking about something and he would say, 'Oh yeah, I know that.' He had this wealth of knowledge that I couldn't understand. I asked Jovan, 'How do you know all this?' And he said that his mom used to read to him when he was a kid."

It wasn't all perfect. Beyond being smart and happy, Jovan had a different side to his personality. Jessyca elaborates: "He was very serious and intense. Part of that was probably from my sadness, because I was, too.

"I remember one time, we were in the car, and Don was singing, 'three blind mice, three blind mice,' and Jo got *mad*, shouting, 'That's not the way you sing it!' He broke down. I was like, 'Ohh, boy!' Don was just laughing. But yeah, Jo was definitely intense.

Very sensitive little boy. There was one time I went to pick him up from school because his teacher called us in and Jo was crying under the desk, because the kids were being mean to him, and he would not come out."

Sheps's experience with Jovan was a little different. As he explains, "He was quiet. He reminds me of a lot of myself, in that sense. He was quiet, and kind of self-content."

The difference in Jovan's personality may speak to how different he was in front of each of his parents. Jovan was one child in front of his father, and another child in front of his mother. That's not unexpected in situations where parents aren't together. Different home, different child.

In Jovan's case, that difference in personality could have been driven by one external influence: Don. A child's relationship with a stepparent can be complicated. And with Don, it was complicated with a capital C! Partly because of Jovan's age, and partly because of the newness of the relationship, things started out well. As Jessyca shares, "They were really close in the beginning. And that's kind of why I liked Don, because Don was really good with Jo. I thought, 'This is the guy I want in his life.' In fact, Don called him *his* son: 'That's my boy, that's my boy. I know that's not my biological son, but that's my boy.'"

But then something changed, specifically with the birth of Jessyca and Don's daughter Lya. Don turned his attention to his biological child, and away from Jovan. Jessyca explains, "At some point he was like, 'I'm not his father, and he shouldn't call me Daddy. He should reserve that for his father, even though I don't like the way Khalil's not really being an active part of his life. I'm going to give it time and let them develop their relationship as time goes by and I'm going to be done.'" Don seemed to feel that there would come a point where Jovan would no longer be his responsibility, even though he, Jessyca, and baby Jo were sharing a home. Over time, Don started to resent Jovan, which started to show in his treatment of his stepchild.

Jessyca says, "He was hard on Jo. He was harder on Jo when Jo got to be about four years old. One time he whooped him with a belt, because Jo had his baby sister on his back, and she fell off. Don lost it. And I knew that was the point where I was like, 'This is not what I want for Jo. This relationship is not going to work.'"

It isn't as simple as it sounds in that story. Don was abusive, in addition to being unfaithful. But like many women in abusive relationships, she stayed. "I thought to myself, 'This man's cheating on me all the time. I'm not going to do this!' But I did, I stayed with Don for years. So, Jo had a rough upbringing at times, watching Don just be terrible to me. He was abusive to me. And then after years went by, he became abusive toward Jo."

The abuse and hostility between Don and Jovan eventually got to the point where it became untenable. Jo began a rotation where he spent some time living with his father, then his grandparents, then his aunt, and on and on. It wasn't until Jessyca and Don finally split that Jovan would move back in with his mother.

While Jessyca and Sheps didn't agree on much when it came to raising baby Jo, they do agree on one thing now, as Sheps explains: "He was definitely loved, spoiled even. Between Jessyca and her parents, her boyfriend, and my parents, my brother, and myself, he definitely got a lot of attention."

Jessyca confirms that. "He was the first baby of my family, so we would all fight for him. Like, 'I get to have the baby tonight!' 'No, *I* get to.' 'Well, he's my baby! I get to have him!' So, I had my sister, my mom, and me all fighting for Jo."

Yvie's memories of their childhood take on a different form, which, as you get to know Yvie, makes perfect sense. When asked about their earliest childhood memories, they spoke about them almost as if they were a theory, and not something they'd lived through. "It always changes, because I don't really . . . I don't know. The earliest parts are such a blur. They're more like bright, colorful paintings."

It's quite common for children to struggle to remember specific details of their childhood. There are a few reasons why that can happen. One is that our brains simply need to make room for more memories, so we dump the oldest ones. Another relates to brain development as we age. And of course, there's trauma: Our brains will block painful memories to protect us from having to experience the emotions all over again. In Yvie's case, it may be a little from each bucket.

As a child, Yvie experienced trauma, without a doubt. Trauma inflicted by Don; from watching their mother being abused; from having two homes, each with different rules; from having parents that subtly or overtly disagreed with one another on how to parent; from having one (or both) parents overshare with them when their little brain couldn't process the information; from being a Black child in America; and from not "fitting in." Take your pick. There was lots of trauma.

The trauma Yvie experienced, while deeply impactful, is unfortunately not unique to them, nor is it uncommon. Lots of kids experience things that can have a negative impact on their psyche, but there are varying degrees of impact. Regardless, trauma can and does influence a child's development. But in Yvie's case, considering everything going on, it's no surprise that the memories are a little fuzzy.

Yvie says, "They're like expressionist paintings. They're ideas more than anything. One that always pops up for me is being at my grandparents' condo, in this little ski town in the mountains in Colorado. And vaguely learning how to swim in the indoor pool and feeling the weird pebble stone pavement underneath my feet. And feeling good about learning how to swim, which then unlocks this other memory of swimming with my aunt in some gigantic space—the biggest pool I'd ever seen—and feeling like I was going to drown. Which unlocks this other memory of being at the ocean. And so, I don't know what my first memory is, but apparently it was when I was wet.

"I think it was very complex to digest, because there's a lot of things that went into my making. I was definitely not a planned child. My mom had me in college. My dad was in college across the country. There was just a bunch of weird factors in my life before I was ever even born. Which meant I grew up in very strange circumstances. My mom was in school for most of my young life. And I halfway lived with my grandparents, and sometimes my aunt would be there. I've always had lots of family around. But also, when you're queer, there's just something different about you that's unexplainable, and I think everybody always loved it, for the most part. But life gets complex as you get older."

The presumption of Yvie's sexuality was apparent from a very young age. As is often the case, mother knew. Jessyca shares, "I think the very first time, he was like . . . oh gosh, one? I had graduated from college, and I was moving out of my parents' house into my own apartment. And we were upstairs going through the attic trying to figure out what things I needed to throw out. I still had Barbies and stuff like that. So, I went up there, and Jo found this old doll of mine that had a missing leg. It was the rattiest-looking doll, one of those dollar-store dolls that my aunt gave me. I hated that doll. I had a Barbie, and I loved that Barbie to death. But Jo wasn't interested in Barbie. He was interested in the doll that had no leg. No leg, funky hair, dollar-store doll, and he loved that doll. He took that doll everywhere he went, and I was like, 'Can we put the doll down now?' And something in me said, 'Hmm, I wonder if there's a possibility he might be gay.' And Don—he was homophobic—was like, 'My boy's not playing with no doll!' And he would try and take the doll away from Jo, and Jo would cry, and cry, and cry, and I would give it back to him.

So, I think I started telling Jo at a very young age that it was okay. I think I asked him a couple of times, because I wanted him to know that I would accept him if he was gay. And I would tell him from time to time, 'You know, if you ever liked boys, I wouldn't be bothered by it. I would still love you. You're still my baby. I want you to feel comfortable being who you are.' So, I kind of knew. Something in me knew."

Sheps concurs. "You know, I might have suspected it, because he never talked about girls or never came home excited by someone in his class. He went to an alternative school, Denver School of the Arts, in middle and most of high school. Part of the conflict that Jessyca and I had at the time was I wanted him to go to a public school, because I felt that while he might have been getting the education he needed, he wasn't getting the social skills. Public schools are rough. Not everyone's the same. When you have to walk down the hall with football players, and basketball players, and wrestlers, and cheerleaders, and all the different groups— there's a whole different vibe that happens—name calling and all that. And you have to learn to survive that, and high school is the place that you learn to survive that.

"Jessyca finally did let him transfer for his senior year. Which I'm very thankful for, because that's when I really saw him blossom in terms of his social life and his creativity. He was in theater, and I remember going to watch him in plays, and stuff like that. He told me he was attracted to boys when he was still in the alternative school. And I remember the conversation very clearly because I asked him, 'Have you ever dated a girl? Are you sure, or are you just curious?' And he was like, 'Well, I'm not sure. But you know, guys pay a lot more attention to me than girls,' was kind of his response, and so I left it at that."

Beyond Don's homophobia, there may have been some subtle attempts to expose Yvie to more traditionally "masculine" activities.

Sam Nobile 🅾 *@onyxfangg*

As Sheps explains, "A lot of folks don't know this, but he grew up camping and fishing a lot. He's probably been on more camping trips than most people." Sheps pauses, then continues. "He hated it. I mean, we'd go fishing, and he liked going to the mountains, and he liked hanging out. But he was the most backflipping, choral-y, handstanding, dancing-around kid I've ever seen. So I would be fishing, and he would be on the shore, looking like he was putting on an ice-skating performance. Or a ballerina, or something like that."

That isn't to say that Sheps was or is homophobic or not supportive of Yvie. Far from it. As he shares, "You know, he was a wonderful kid, and being gay did not change that. He was still the same genius, creative, happy kid that he was before he told me. I don't know if I was worried, I just thought it was a far cry from me, because I was a hound. I remember when he finally did come out and tell me, and in my crude way I said, 'Oh. Well, that's more for me.' I said that in front of him, and we sat and laughed about it."

Yvie's awareness of their sexuality and gender began at a fairly early age. "I was a horny kid. A lot of my early memories are of playing around with other boys *and* girls. It was like, 'Wow, I want to see what your parts are' and 'Look at my parts' and 'What do yours feel like? What do mine feel like? What's going on?' And it was always taboo, because of course nobody wants little kids to be fucking around."

Yvie wasn't having sex, nor are they suggesting that young children having sex is a good thing. Not in the way adults have sex. Yvie was a curious child, like most children are. They see their own bodies and then they see the bodies of others, and they have a genuine curiosity. It's natural. Admittedly, Yvie may have been a little more sexually curious than other children, but they're not an anomaly.

"I liked playing with kids and we'd all play together and do little kid shit. But the best game that we played was whenever we just took our clothes off. I didn't even understand what it was making me feel about two human beings naked next to each other. But it was something that happened in so many of my friendships, at least up to a certain point. Because at a certain point in your life, you learn it's not okay to be sexual with other people, especially if they're a certain sex. So, you just stop. You start internalizing all of those urges, those desires. Until you go through puberty, and you learn the source of all those feelings."

This is where the theme of shame shows up in our story. And it's a theme that will come up a few times over the course of Yvie's life. We teach our children shame by negatively reacting to their behavior, like when a child is curious about their body or others' bodies, and we tell them that's wrong. That's what happened with Yvie. "If you tell a child they can't do something, they're going to want to do it twice as much. So, a lot of my early childhood memories are of fooling around with little boys, little girls, all the other kids. That started when I was old enough to understand that if you do things, you have to do them secretly, and you have to be ashamed of them."

There were several instances in Yvie's childhood where the reaction to their behavior reinforced a sense of shame. Like one instance during nap time at day care, where Yvie and another boy were lying together, playing with each other's bodies. The teacher's reaction of shock and disgust made it clear to Yvie that what they were doing was something to be ashamed of. That feeling was reinforced when Yvie's entire family—parents, grandparents, uncles, and aunts—learned about what happened. Yvie's family didn't know what to think. Yvie wasn't an abnormal child, but Yvie was marching to the beat of their own drum.

That uniqueness was on display very early on and continued all the way through high school and beyond. For some it was a repellent—a reason to ostracize Yvie—but for others it's what attracted them to Yvie. Teena was one of the latter. Yvie met **Teena** at DSA, and they became immediate best friends, which they are to this day. Teena describes their first encounter: "I was so obsessed with X-Men that I was hand-sewing X-Men dolls, and they had changeable outfits. And most important, the show had this unique and recognizable theme music. One day, I'm sitting in art class, and I hear someone humming that theme song, and I was like, 'Who else here is obsessed with X-Men? I thought that was just me.' And I look over and it's Jovan." And a friendship was born.

Yvie and Teena had more in common than just Professor Xavier and his school for gifted youngsters. As Teena says, "We both were kind of misfits, which is weird to say, being a misfit at an art school. But I kind of have a feeling it's because we both weren't quite as rich as most of the kids. There were a lot of rich kids at that school, and I don't think either of us were fitting in very well."

There's one other little detail about Yvie: They love to bend and flip, as both Sheps and Jessyca shared. Anyone who has ever seen Yvie perform knows that, because they're regularly contorted into a pretzel. Sheps and Jessyca would let young Jovan watch ice skating on television, and as Jo grew up, they would try and imitate the moves of the skaters, albeit on carpet. That fascination with movement carried on throughout Yvie's life.

Even Yvie's DSA teacher Deb Rosenbaum saw it. "Jo was very kinetic. The school has a big rotunda in the front. Our door to the visual arts studio was right off that rotunda, and he used to go out there and just do flips and all kinds of dance moves. Numerous times the dance department tried to get him to come over to dance and he said he didn't want to do that. We just couldn't believe the athleticism and the flexibility that he had."

The close relationship between Teena and Yvie gave Teena a front-row seat to observe Yvie, and Teena saw a different side to Yvie's behavior. "It seemed like Jovan was always trying to fit in with the popular boys. And I'm not sure if they were making fun of him or not, but I definitely felt like there was a power dynamic there that was not very fun to watch. I think there was maybe some underlying racism at our school as well. The White kids were definitely making fun of the Black kids. Jovan was very outgoing, very loud. Always doing things to impress people, telling funny jokes or raising his hand in class and saying something kind of smart. There were these boys that Jovan was always trying to impress, they were the popular dudes in the art class. And I remember all these times I'd be looking out on the field and Jovan's doing a backflip just to impress them." That's a theme that we'll see more of—Yvie's need to impress other people, likely stemming from a lack of self-esteem. Yvie wanted people to like them. They were a young, queer, Black child struggling to fit in, trying to figure out who they were. Add to that the trauma of childhood, and a high sex drive, and we get what we get.

There's one last layer that is critically important in defining Yvie: pain. What no one knew at the time was that Jovan has hypermobile Ehlers-Danlos syndrome (hEDS), a connective-tissue disorder that affects the joints and skin. People with hEDS have overly flexible joints and stretchy skin. All that flipping and twisting was causing Yvie pain. And the only solution to hEDS is to take glucosamine and hope for the best. There is no cure.

Let's recap on who baby Jo was: happy, serious, intense, very sexual, bending and flipping, traumatized, and living with a chronic illness that left them in constant pain. Jovan's childhood was filled with love and joy, and pain and sorrow. They had a far from average childhood. In some ways, Yvie was just an average kid who wanted to run and play, yet they were clearly destined for fame. When you add all the pieces together, it's clear that the early days of Yvie's life were filled with challenges that would leave many scarred. But all of those experiences are what put Yvie on their path toward superstardom, and without them, Yvie Oddly would not be who they were destined to be.

YVIE'S TOP 5 FAVORITE MOVIE MONSTERS

1. The monster from *It Follows*: Specifically as the tall and conspicuous man with menacing dark circles under his eyes. I felt seen.

2. Audrey II from *Little Shop of Horrors*: I haven't bought a plant since.

3. Idris Elba and Judy Dench in *Cats*: That movie itself was a monster.

4. The Creatures from *A Quiet Place*: John Krasinski ain't right.

5. Matt Gaetz or Marjorie Taylor Greene tie for fifth: It's a tossup.

CHAPTER 2

ADAM AND YVIE: COMING OUT

Every LGBTQIA+ person's coming out story is unique, but many kids follow a relatively similar path: At some point a person realizes they're not quite like everyone else. That difference may be their sexuality, or their gender, or both. And for kids—and really for anyone—being different is the last thing they want. Being different makes them stand out, and standing out can lead to bullying, ostracism, and discrimination. In some instances, they may not really have a choice because their sexuality or gender is too difficult to hide, and people will make assumptions. But in some cases, people may suppress who they are, as hard as they can, in order to fit in. And that can lead to a plethora of problems, not the least of which is feelings of shame.

Yvie's story is no different. "The thoughts have always been there. I've always known that I was attracted to other guys. But I started realizing that it was a specific part of my sexuality, and not something that every boy feels. Because I fooled around with lots of kids who turned out to be straight, there was this point where it became clear: 'Oh, no, I'm the only one having these thoughts about boys. That probably means that some part of me is gay.' And that started happening in middle school. But that's also when I still believed I had the power to fight them. So, it was the typical story of 'I'd pray to God to take away my gayness.'"

This is a pretty common narrative in someone's coming out: shame, brought on by religious teachings. Not all religions are homophobic, mind you, but there are still some that have a very negative approach to sexuality and gender. Yvie was raised in a fairly religious family. Messages that your sexuality is a deviance, brought on by unseen evil powers, can be an enormous burden to carry. "Shame formed a lot of my identity," Yvie says. "Not even just sexually, but learning how to navigate the world as a mixed-race, gender-queer, generally queer adult in a White, Midwestern city is its own form of constantly feeling shamed for being who you are. I recently remembered that after a certain point in my life, when kids would start being assholes (like kids are) and start picking on me for things, one of the things that really stuck with me was my lips. They'd always call me fish-lips, and gap tooth, and Bugs Bunny. And I remember practicing in the mirror, pursing my lips to make them smaller when I met people. The other day, when somebody walked into the same elevator that I was in, I caught myself doing it still, pursing my lips to make them smaller. I don't know if it's to make others feel comfortable, or if it's just out of habit. But I remember that's where it started, being like, 'Okay, make your face more normal. Be very ashamed of who you are, for things you can't change.' Well, at least not without lots of money and plastic surgery."

Imagine adjusting or hiding an aspect of your identity, as many readers will have tried. Desperately trying to mask part of who you are—something that is just part of your existence—so you stand out less. And that's with just one identity. Now add the intersections of identity that Yvie experiences—mixed race, Black (but Black enough?), gender queer, sexually queer, and living with a chronic illness. That level of suppression is bound to come with a boatload of shame.

"I remember I would make deals with God after I would watch gay porn. I'd be like, 'Okay. Well, I did it. And I promise I won't do it again . . . for a month.' It's all that reconciling that happened in middle school that I realized that there was something there."

Eventually, as Yvie progressed through high school, they started to come to terms with their identity. "That was the actual embracing of it and being like, 'Yes, okay. This is who I am.' That was like, age fifteen, even if I didn't tell anyone that it's a part of me. And it was because I was in a friend group where literally in one year, five of us came out as bisexual. So, the first person did it, and it was like, 'Wow! That's so shocking. A real-life bisexual person I'm actually already friends with.' And I think the last person to have come out to me was my girlfriend at the time, while we were dating. And she was like, 'Yeah, I'm bisexual.' And that's when I was like, 'Wait. If this girl who's dating me can also admit that she likes girls, maybe I can do the same.'"

Like many, Yvie started to come to terms with their identity because of a boy in their friend group whom they had a crush on, who had also come out as bisexual. "I was like, 'Oh my God, maybe this is it. This is what I've needed to come to terms with everything. I'm just gonna tell this boy how I feel about him, and he's gonna hold me in his arms and do whatever we do as teenage boys.' And so, he was the first person I came out to."

Ultimately, in true after-school-special fashion, the boy turned out to have feelings for someone else. "He was very sweet. He was like, 'Well, I know how scary this is. I'm here for you, and I really like you. But I actually like somebody else now.'" Yvie was devastated, as any newly minted teenage bisexual would be.

Sadly, coming out doesn't magically make everything better. It's like taking the lid off a boiling pot. Sure, it stops the steam from blowing out the sides, but it doesn't stop the water from boiling. "It's not like the shame was lifted. It was more like one tiny cinder block was taken off my shoulders, out of the giant pile of bricks I was carrying. It was like, 'Well, I no longer have to lie to myself about this. But now I probably have to lie to the world.' When I had initially come out, I had plans for myself. I was like, 'Okay, so you're just going to play it cool, and play it straight through high school. And then when you get to college you can finally have sex with guys and live that life because everyone does that in college. And then you're going to get married to a nice woman and have a few kids.'"

Yvie Oddly with a wife and kids. That is difficult to visualize. But the point is, even in 2009 at the age of fifteen, sex with men was okay, but the idea of being in a committed relationship with someone was going to involve a woman. Because that's what society expects and what is presented everywhere you turn. Most people believe (and there's research to support this) that coming out today (or in 2009) is easy and isn't an issue. But is that true? It's true that it's easier to come out now than it was twenty-plus years ago, but there are still segments of society that hate queer people.

"That's the strangest part about it. There was still so much acceptance around me. I went to school at 'DS Gay.' And my mom asked me if I was gay long before I really understood what the concept was. So, there was support around me. But I still grew up in a world where that was not the case. You can have a gay TV show, but that doesn't mean it's okay for you to actually go walking around your small town with a swish in your hips. So, the hardest part about it, for me, was having the perception of me changed. I didn't want my friends to treat me like I was gay. I remember, because as I started coming out to friends, I would have a very serious conversation with them. I'd be like, 'Yes, I'm bisexual. But I'm really afraid to tell people, and I don't want to because I don't want them to treat me differently and think of me differently.' Even if it was in a positive way, I didn't want people to treat me like a 'gay person.' I didn't want the girls in my life to be like, 'Yes, let's go shopping! Let's talk about boys, and you can give me advice.' And there were girls who did that, and it was my worst nightmare come true. But that's also because even in accepting that I liked boys, I was so fucking homophobic. The first conversations I had about liking boys were like, 'Yeah, I like boys. But like, real boys.'"

Now we get to the part where the shame transitions into internalized homophobia. That's when you acknowledge and accept your sexuality, but you hate yourself for it. Like when you think frosted tips will make you look cool, but you realize it just makes you look like an asshole, but you leave them in because your mom spent a lot of money on them. Internalized homophobia can lead to depression, anxiety, substance abuse, self-harm, suicidal ideation, and even violence toward other LGBTQIA+ people. It's long been suspected—and there's some recent research that supports this—that those who are the most ardently anti-LGBTQIA+ are actually themselves LGBTQIA+, albeit in denial or deeply closeted.

One way people's internalized homophobia manifests can be in something called toxic masculinity. That feels like it needs a definition. So we will turn to Wikipedia:

> *Toxic masculinity is a set of certain male behaviors associated with harm to society and men themselves. Stereotypical aspects of traditional masculinity, such as social dominance, misogyny, and homophobia can be considered "toxic" due in part to their promotion of violence, including sexual assault and domestic violence. Socialization of boys often normalizes violence, such as in the saying "boys will be boys" about bullying and aggression.*

Applied to people within the LGBTQIA+ communities, it's okay to acknowledge you are attracted to men (if you identify as a man), but you're only going to be attracted to guys who are hyper-masculine, as was Yvie's experience when they first came out. "I didn't like all these skinny, pretty, Abercrombie & Fitch–wearing, nice clothes–dressing boys. I wanted a man's man, you know? I remember that in the same year that I came out, I told this boy— let's call him Zeus—that I loved him and he was like, 'Oh, too late.' There was another gay guy—let's call this one Hera—who started hanging out with my best friend, and Zeus and Hera were a thing. And I hated Hera. I hate, hate, hated him. Probably a little bit because of jealousy, or whatever. But also, I hated him because he was so gay. He was like, 'Yeah, oh my God. Did you watch *Gossip Girl* last night? It was so good.' He was a vocal major, which meant he was a gay major too. I remember being disgusted by him. And he was so attracted to me. But after coming out and realizing who I was, or at least starting to, he was in the year of first kisses. And he wanted to sleep with me. I could have had the experience I had dreamed of, having weird teenage sex, losing my virginity to a guy. He was really gorgeous, too, but he was too gay for me."

So where does that come from? How does someone get to a point where they can acknowledge that their sexuality is not exclusively heterosexual, but they develop a loathing for men who aren't masculine? Where does one develop internalized homophobia?

According to Yvie, "A lot of the hatred I had for femininity, specifically in boys, came from learning it from my stepdad."

Ah yes. Don. We'd forgotten about Don. Not surprisingly, he had more of an impact that we might have suspected. Our perspectives are shaped by the people in our lives. As children, we learn from our parents, siblings, extended family, teachers, and even friends. Children model the behavior they see around them, even if they reject that behavior. Homophobia, biphobia, and transphobia are learned behaviors. No child wakes up feeling that way. They witness it in others. While Yvie's relationship with Don was tumultuous and even violent, Don's overt homophobic beliefs impacted them. There is no love lost between Yvie and Don, it's fair to say, but Don's historical behavior impacted Yvie as they started to explore their sexual orientation, whether Yvie liked it or not.

"I don't think it's one hundred percent right or fair to blame somebody else for the things you see, feel, or think. But, after doing some mental digging, I remember a lot of my first very homophobic experiences coming from my stepdad. My mom was always supportive, but she was with this guy who came from Texas. Don was a cowboy, he was a pilot, he used to be in the army, he was a man's man. And one of my earlier memories was him watching this game show where they had a bunch of different little games in it, and you could win lots of money. And one of the games was they had a bunch of women on stage, and it was a guy's job to try and figure out which of these women were women, and which of these women were men. So, here's the social context of like, 'Uh-oh, some weird trannies are trying to sneak around and be a part of our society.' And I remember how disgusted he was by them. He was like, 'Oh, these fucking RuPauls on my screen. I don't care how much money they'd give me; I wouldn't get within ten feet of them.' And then there's a time where we were going to eat at an Applebee's, and I don't even know if the server was gay or Trans, because I don't remember the person who triggered it. But I remember our waiter being so effeminate, or so Trans, or so whatever, that my stepdad made us leave. Not even like, 'Oh, can we have another server?'—the backhanded, nice, polite way of saying, 'I hate that person.' We had to leave the whole-ass establishment."

Yvie continued their journey of coming out. "I came out to my friends at the end of our school year—I can't remember if it was freshman or sophomore. And by the time school had started again in August, my mom knew, my dad knew, and then within the year after that, basically everyone in my life knew. I did not get any of the worst of the worst. I didn't get anyone who was like, 'Get the fuck out, you're disowned!'"

Not surprisingly, Yvie shares that their coming out wasn't as "traditional" as some others. For many people, when they come out to a family member, there's usually tears and (hopefully) a lot of hugging and "I still love you just the way you are" type of comments. Not for Yvie. "It's funny because a lot of my coming outs happened in arguments, like with my mom. I came out to her because I had hung out with my uncle and told him something I didn't tell her. And she was like, 'You don't even love me anymore! You would tell your uncle everything before you told me.' And I was like, 'Yeah, Mom? Well, I'm bisexual!' My dad, I told after my sister told him. And he was like, 'Are you sure there isn't anything you want to tell me?' And we got into a little argument.

So that was another coming out argument. My stepdad and I were in a pretty serious argument, and he told me I was acting like a wussy, like a little fairy. And I was like, 'Well, you know what, Don? I am a fairy. I'm gay.' He's actually the first person I ever said gay to because it's a lot easier than saying bisexual. And I think it had more of a punch to it. But their responses were still pretty filled with love. My dad was like, 'I love you no matter what.' My mom was like, 'I love you no matter what. But I think you're going to hell still. And it's not your fault; some people are just born to go to hell.'

"A lot of my coming out still comes with, not shame, but the feeling of deviancy. And this is punctuated most by me coming out to my granddad. I remember around the end of my year of coming out, I came out to my granddad because he was like, 'Are you gay?' And I was like, 'No, I'm bisexual.' And he was just like, 'Okay. Well just don't tell your nana, she couldn't handle it.' And I was like, 'Okay, well, there's a little bit of shame in that.' And he was like, 'Just promise me that because you're breaking all these rules because you're gay, that you won't get into drugs, and all that other bad shit too. You've still got to be good with God.' And that's what stuck with me, is this equation of gayness and deviancy. And he understood it better than I ever could have, until I was an adult. Being the deviant, doing drugs, was like, 'You know what? I like doing things that I'm not supposed to. I enjoy it.'" I feel like that exchange would be really well done with puppets. Because everybody loves puppets.

Let's unpack this, because this is another one of those important character-defining plot points: Yvie and authority. We need to look at this because it's something that has come up in Yvie's public life, including their time on *Drag Race*. The simple truth is that Yvie has issues with authority figures. That started at a young age, where they would push back against the authority figures in their life. They like to argue and challenge, which we saw on season 11 of *Drag Race*. That behavior stems from their primary examples of authority—their parents—who practiced a "do what I say, not what I do" approach to parenting. "Mom would tell me, 'You can't have tantrums out in public. It's not right. You have to behave better.' Even though the week prior, her and my dad were literally screaming in the middle of the street at each other." That example has led Yvie to take on a perpetual position of challenger, which continues to this day. We see that in their art. Yvie continues to push back against societal expectations.

There is an old perception—wildly inaccurate—that when a person comes out as bisexual, it's just the dress rehearsal before they come out as gay or lesbian. Some see it as a "safe" identity, before fully stepping into the community. That is completely incorrect, and bisexual and pansexual people do exist. Yet, Yvie described themselves as bisexual, and not gay . . . for the most part. Unless they were trying to shock Don. Which begs the question, does Yvie *still* identify as bisexual? "I think there are parts of me that still are. There is still something innately hot to me about a naked woman. And also, in the queering of gender that has happened within my lifetime, it's really hard to be like, 'Yes, I only like *men* who have to be *real men*.' Because what the fuck is a real man? It's hard for me to even describe myself as gay

David Gump-Holmes 📷 *@whaddupholmess*

anymore because I'm like, 'You don't have to have the same bits and bobbits as me.' I thought I was bisexual for the longest of times; now I'm queer leaning gay. Gay for straight people, queer for people who get it."

Like many people in the LGBTQIA+ community, Yvie has gone through an evolution with their identity. "Since embracing that I was anywhere under our rainbow umbrella, I've gone through lots of transformations about how I feel about my identity. First, obviously, there was the shame, guilt, shut-up-and-hide-it phase. And then I remember going to my first Pride. I remember going out to a club for the first time as an eighteen-year-old, my first hook-ups. These things helped me transform from being a person who is ashamed to a person who is militantly proud, the peacocking twink. And that's when I started testing boundaries. I remember the first time I really started getting in trouble in my senior year at my new school was not because of my bad grades, even though they were there. Not because of my sassy mouth, even though it was there. It was because I kept breaking their dress code rules." Denver East High School has a dress code that is quite extensive, and some might call it subjective and restrictive.

"I got detention at the end of my senior year because I kept breaking dress code rules. That's when my mind had switched and actually begun to take in what would be the foundation of my understanding of drag. Which is, that how you present yourself in the world is one of the most important things. It is how people identify with you before they ever say a word. And so, after a social experiment of dressing in all black for a week and having all the emo kids talk to me, and then dressing preppy for a week and suddenly having all these preppy bitches being cool with me, I realized that if I ever want gay people to see me and to have a gay experience, I needed to start getting gayer. So, it was crop tops, and short shorts, and see-through this and that. And I started shopping in the women's section because that's where expression was allowed. Men have T-shirts and pants. In the women's section you could get a blouse. And it's just revealing enough to make your teacher pull you out of class."

So little Jovan evolved from his internalized homophobia into queer with a capital Q. This is what is referred to as "context," because it's the evolution of how Jovan became Yvie. Or more to the point, how Yvie came bursting out of Jovan. "After high school, the first community members that I really got to find and bond with were just other bitchy twinks. So, I remember feeling so good about having this full circle. I used to be this ugly duckling who people didn't want to date, and I couldn't get guys to fuck me. Then it went to being one of the hot twinks in our group of racially diverse twinks from around the world. I was hot Black twink, and we had hot Asian twink, and then we had this weird brunette twink. And it felt cool to have a community within the community, and to have our primary objective be, 'Be as gay as possible.' When we'd hang out, we'd walk down the streets with the shortest of shorts, with the swishiest of hips, singing Lady Gaga, and that felt so good. For the first time in my life, it felt good to be feminine. All the traits that I had associated with bad, that people had told me were weird, or that I should stop doing as a kid—the playing with dolls, the crossing your legs, the limpness of the wrists—were all things that I could be celebrated for. So, in a way, it was exploring my gender identity. But honestly, what really did chip away at that shame, truly, was drag."

YVIE'S TOP 5 FAVORITE READS FROM *RUPAUL'S DRAG RACE* (USA)

1. "I know we all read her for those kitten heels but it's not her fault—they start off as stilettos." Loosey LaDuca to Mistress Isabelle Brooks on season 15.

2. "Girl I love you but your career only has movement because the earth has to spin on its axis." Blair St. Clair to Mariah Paris Balenciaga on *All Stars*, season 5.

3. "Shangela! You have come so far! Initially, your makeup was kind of busted and your outfits were a mess and your personality was super grating, but look how far you've come now. You are much older." BenDeLaCrème to Shangela on *All Stars*, season 3.

4. "Adore. I know what you got on your SATs. Ketchup." Bianca Del Rio to Adore Delano on season 6.

5. "LaLa Ri, bitch this look is sickening girl . . . is something nobody said to you in the ball challenge." Rosé to LaLa Ri, season 13.

CHAPTER 3

DRAGGED ACROSS CONCRETE: THE BIRTH OF YVIE ODDLY

How is a drag queen born? Everyone's journey is different. For some, it starts with a dare on Halloween where you get done up in something you buy at a secondhand shop. For some, it's a deliberate moment—for whatever reason—where you have decided that you don't want to just *try* being in drag; you want to *be* a drag queen. For Yvie, their foray into drag started as part of their coming out as LGBTQIA+ and exploring their gender.

"It was within my first year of being out that I started drag. I fell in love with it and saw it as this secret way to express the girly parts of me that I had always had. To get to play dress-up in my little sister's clothes, and my mom's makeup and heels. So, there was the first initial thought of 'doing drag would be fun.' There was the first time buying heels, and then being the twink in our friend group who could walk in heels, and who would wear heels for a night out on the town. And then there was the first time I was like, 'Wait, I want to do some drag. I'm going to buy a whole face full of makeup.' And then there's the first step of leaving the house in drag. All of those happened within one year of adulthood: buying my heels, thinking about doing drag, deciding to try it out once while watching *Drag Race*, painting my face. And then getting to this place where, on Valentine's Day of 2012, my school was putting on a show and Venus D-Lite was going to be there, and I was going to officially do drag . . . in public."

Venus D-Lite was a contestant on *RuPaul's Drag Race* season 3. And while she tragically was sent home first, she continues to be an icon in the community and is an amazing performer and impersonator, including doing the best Madonna impersonation outside of the real Madonna.

For Yvie, that night was the beginning of their future. As they explain, "I used that show as my springboard to get up the courage to leave my house in drag. And I remember trying to sneak past my dad without him seeing my face, because I was living at his house at the time. And he was like, 'What are you doing?' And I was like, 'Oh, going to school.' And his girlfriend at the time was like, 'Well, just be careful because the queens out there can be very mean.' Which, now I see as her being like, 'Bitch, you look busted.' I had actually gotten up super early that day to paint my face so I could go downtown and get an outfit to perform in. And so, in full makeup, I went into a Ross store, which was right near my campus, and shopped for my first drag dress half an hour before I had to be in class.

"It was such a terrifying day. Especially because I didn't realize how traumatic it was to jump from no drag into doing daytime drag, going to my classes, walking around campus in drag. I just kicked the door open, and all of those fears also fed me because it felt like I was in control of the eyes on me. There is this same concept that I have been playing with for a while, of dressing up, and dressing out, to intentionally attract attention, instead of them looking at me because I was naturally a little bit gay, or a little bit funny looking. It was embracing it and being like, 'Yes, I am wearing an entirely see-through outfit. And yes, I do have my nails painted. And yes, I am dressed in booty shorts in the middle of January.' It was a very intentional 'I'm going to be here to fuck up your visual day. And if you're looking at me because I'm weird, it's because I chose it.' And it just felt like everybody was staring at me, which they probably were because I was like six and a half feet tall, looked terrible, and was wearing a Ross dress. But this was an exhilarating moment because it was like, 'Yeah, this is why I'm here. I am a woman, and I am buying this dress for myself.' And also, 'I don't know if I can afford it.'"

Venus remembers Yvie from that fateful night so many years ago. "After the show, we had agreed to do a meet and greet with the students. I remember there was this really, really tall drag baby that came up to me and she said she loved the show, and she adored me on *Drag Race* and was very honored to meet me. And I looked at Yvie and there was something so unique about them, and I had this really strong premonition and feeling that something was coming for them. I couldn't really explain it, but I just had a feeling. And I told Yvie, 'I really see great things for you in the future. Something big is coming for you.'"

And that was the birth of the queen that is now Yvie, walking around the campus of Metropolitan State University of Denver in day drag in a dress from Ross that they probably couldn't afford. But they were a long way from drag superstardom. That day, February 14, 2012, little baby Yvie took to the stage for the first time, performing "Scheiße" (which is German for "fuck") by Lady Gaga from her iconic 2011 *Born This Way* album.

"I chose it because it was dancy, and fun, and it felt gay. And at that time my body felt invincible. I was like, 'I might not know a lot about drag but I can walk in heels, and I can do backflips in heels.' It was basically just one big shit show if I look back on it now. My wig fell off, my Ross dress was getting caught up in my heels. And for some strange reason I felt like my outfit wasn't complete unless I was also wearing pants, because I was like, 'I'm going to break gender norms. I don't just wear dresses, I wear dresses over my jeans.' But I got to combine all of the things that I had ever really loved before: the praise, the attention, the shock and awe of having somebody see you do a flip for the first time *and* do it in heels or jumping off a stage. It felt like being a daredevil, because everyone was gasping. And after my performance, I had such a long line of people who I both knew and didn't know just being like, 'That was so amazing.' And for me, the extra gratification was that there were also one or two local, seasoned queens who were hired to come in and perform in the show. And I was like, 'Bitch, I just outperformed the local queens.'"

Yvie came away from that moment with a huge burst of confidence. "I left thinking, 'I think I have to do this seriously now.' And one of my friends who I hung out with in the LGBT office at school told me that the LGBT center [called The Center on Colfax] had a youth program for people up to age twenty-two, and they did monthly drag shows. And that's when I started attending those and doing drag. Once a month I would do drag."

But Yvie still wasn't quite Yvie yet. "At first, I performed under the name Avon LaRue. That's because the only wig that I owned was a short red bob. And then I got a dress from Macy's that was red. I like the color red, but it was a pun on the fact that I'm a street-walking hooker, but also that I'm wearing lots of red." For clarity, in French "LaRue" means "the street," or more specifically refers to someone who lives beside a road, track, or pathway. Not important, but interesting.

So, if that's where the last name came from, where did Avon come from? "This is where I think it starts to become an interesting exploration of my own identity as maybe a Trans person. I wanted a name that sounded like my name. And my name, to me, always sounded like it could be masculine or feminine. But I didn't want to be myself, so there had to be one degree of separation. For me, Avon was perfect because it took almost all of the letters in my name and just scrambled them a little bit. And it's also a makeup, so I was like, 'Drag queens have to have a makeup name, you have to have a pun, you have to be French.' Avon LaRue is literally all of that: It's a makeup name; it's the separation of me, but still a name I could recognize; and it's a red hooker."

The name Avon LaRue didn't last. Sometimes queens pick a name and stick with it. Sometimes, it's an evolution. "I had started going to these tiny little drag shows in the basement of The Center. That was the first time seeing more drag culture. And I thought, 'Well, I just kind of chose my last name because I had a red dress and I liked red. But I don't want to be tied to red forever. What's something that's even stronger for me?' I really liked the V in Avon and Jovan. And so, I was like, 'Well, what about Eve? Because Eve was the first woman. And Eve is also nighttime, so it's dark and I am a dark, mysterious woman. And Avon can stay because you still need a makeup.' When I finally graduated from performing in the basement to performing in a bar, I was Avon Eve.

"The hard part is I wasn't even twenty-one yet. And in Denver it's hard to do a whole lot if you're not old enough to go into the bars. But somebody had come to one of our shows at The Center and she ran a competition every Monday. It was a 'win a bar tab' or something-type contest. Nothing major. And she was like, 'Oh my God, you're so fantastic. I can tell you're a baby queen, but this is a good place to come and gain some experience. You should come and start doing my competition on Mondays.' When she asked how old I was, I told her twenty-one, and nobody at the bar ever checked my ID, or I'd say I left it at home. And I'm in drag, so I'd say, 'I'm performing tonight but I don't know where my ID is.' So, the first year of my drag career was sneaking into this club."

Being underage was one thing, but Yvie was also dealing with some real-life challenges to their success. "At this point I wasn't even living in Denver. I had gotten kicked out of my mom's house for smoking pot and fucking up in school. I had moved in with one of my former roommates in their parents' basement out in Lakewood, Colorado. For context, I lived in a place called Green Mountain, which you might imagine was a mountain, and Denver is not in the mountains. And I didn't have a car. I was shit broke, busing two hours to go to school, to go to my shitty retail job, to go to the city and be gay. So, I would bus for two hours in drag from suburbia on a mountain through the inner-city streets of downtown Denver. And then go to this bar and perform, and hopefully win a fifty-dollar drink tab. And when it was over, I'd have to sleep on the streets until the buses started running again. Or a few times, when it was really cold, I walked all the way across Denver and broke into my mom's house to sleep. And that is the beginning: It's my drag feeding itself from the scraps I can afford to spare from my life. And I remember early on, realizing that if I wanted to have cool things like all the other drag queens did, I was going to have to make them. So, I started making outfits."

As we know from *Drag Race* season 11, young Yvie didn't know how to sew, but that doesn't mean they weren't a crafty queen. Yvie was a visual artist, and that skill would come in handy as they were developing their drag aesthetic. Yvie started to evolve their drag from straight off the rack to something more conceptual. "I would save all my money to go to Goodwill and all these thrift stores at Halloween and get their costume-iest costume clothes. And then take a hot glue gun and some scissors and just start fucking with them. Or the primitive version of trying to stone them, or add fringe, or just do whatever to make them feel that much more like drag and less like clothing."

At this point in Yvie's journey, they were still nowhere near superstardom, let alone actually being Yvie. Many queens go through a process of developing. It can be a long road from that first moment in drag to being a recognizable drag star. The bedroom queens, who arrive on *Drag Race* with six months' experience, having never been on a stage, are a rarity. Yvie was following their own path, which had a lot of twists and turns. "There are steps I had to complete to get into the Denver scene. And at that time, the best way to get into the Denver scene was through these competition shows."

Let's paint a picture. It's Monday night in Denver—which isn't exactly the hottest night of the week in gay bars—and there's a drag competition, but the bar is practically empty. Now drop Yvie into that scenario. "It's a big, empty bar. We're not talking New York here. It's a space with four or five people in it. And you're giving everything trying to make them all scream. So, there's that competition and other competitions like that around Denver, which had small followings. And then there was Denver's biggest gay club—the first place I ever got to go out and be gay—Tracks."

A friend of Yvie's took them to Tracks for a *Drag Race* viewing party—season 5, aka Monsoon Season—where they learned about

Ylan AKFLY @ylanakfly

another drag contest. "There was a contest called Ultimate Queen, which was the biggest contest in Denver. It got you on the biggest stage at the biggest club, literally on stage right next to the Ru girls who would come and perform at that time. I saw that and was like, 'Oh my God, I have to do it. I have to win, and I have to get there.' So within the year of Avon Eve coming into her own, I tried out for Ultimate Queen. And it's one of the biggest heartbreaks that fueled my career for a long time. Because I tried out, and it had two weeks of auditions. I did my thing the first week, and everybody was blown away. Nina Flowers was one of the judges at the time and was like, 'He has no car, that's so amazing. You're going to go far.'"

Some readers may not actually know who Nina Flowers is, which is shocking and a little sad. Nina is one of the original Ru girls, and the first contestant from Denver, although originally from Puerto Rico. Nina appeared on season 1 of *RuPaul's Drag Race* (yes, the season with the really bad lighting) way back in 2009. Nina finished second and was named Miss Congeniality. Not surprisingly, a lot of queens in Denver looked up to Nina because they were one of the first celebrity queens to come out of *Drag Race*. Yvie admired Nina even more because her style of drag was unique. Nina's recollection of Yvie's first audition for Ultimate Queen echoes Yvie's: "I was immediately captivated by their uniqueness and stage presence. They had that 'It' factor from day one."

The second week of auditions did not go as well. Ultimate Queen follows a similar model to *The Voice*. A judge has to pick you for their team. Unfortunately for Yvie, Nina wasn't on the judging panel for week two. "I did this song that I really wanted to perform but that honestly was such a buzzkill, especially in a night-club atmosphere. And so, no matter how many tricks I pulled, no matter what I did, I couldn't get any of the judges to pick me for their teams to be in the competition."

Nina saw what was happening, and as much as she tried to influence the other judges, no one bit because they didn't see Yvie's potential. "Yvie didn't get picked because none of the judges that were on the panel had the experience to recognize what Yvie represented, what they had to offer. In my opinion, the judges were focusing on traditional drag, and not on the fresh, the different, and the out of the box. Yes, Yvie needed work in some areas. But makeup, you can learn. Wardrobe you can work on. Now, talent . . . you are either born with it or you aren't. I remember being furious at the judges for not picking them. I will never forget, I walked up to Yvie without knowing them and said, 'These judges don't know shit, they don't know what they are missing.' And I was right. They came back the following year and took the competition by storm. Yvie knows exactly who they are as an artist, and they bring it every time."

Yvie didn't get down about it. They used that moment of loss as a spark to drive them, and to keep on pushing forward toward their goal. "And so in that last year of Avon Eve, I did all the little competitions around Denver, specifically with the intent of getting better, looking better, and performing better for the people. When Ultimate Queen rolled around again, I realized that I had to take this seriously if I wanted to break in. Not only would I have to perform and look good, but I'd have to be someone who is such an identity that people want to book them or throw dollars at them. I had already been performing for two or three years, so I'd heard everybody and their mother be like, 'Bitch, you're so weird, you're such a weirdo. The way your body moves is so strange.' So, I decided to change my name for the purpose of going into this competition like a strong competitor and a strong queen. I had already built a little bit of a name as Avon Eve, so it was funny to watch the judges try and grasp me as this new idea, as Yvie Oddly, as an entity that was here specifically to feed the weird."

And so in the spring of 2015, Avon Eve retired and Yvie Oddly was officially born, and the audience ate it up! "Whatever I was doing at that time really struck a chord with people. In thirteen weeks of competing, I ended up building a really strong following, fan base, friends, and supporters in Denver. Simply because they were so excited for there to be a queen who wasn't about doing lots of hair flips, and cackity cacks, and snick snack to the 5-6-7-8 in a sparkly body suit. But to get booked at the shows, you really did have to be one of the girls in the prominent drag houses at the time, which we're all like, 'Fish, yes. We're fish. Fish is everything.'"

"Fish" is a term used to describe a queen who looks and acts like a woman to the extent that people might not know they weren't assigned female at birth. It's not a terribly kind term and has fallen out of usage.

"So, it was a really big shake-up, I think, for the culture of Denver drag, because while there were people who would do weird things before me, there was no space for weird girls. There were no bookings for people who were going to consistently come out and freak them out. I had some people who tried to get me in their house."

The concept of "houses" or "families" came out of the Ballroom Scene of the 1960s and '70s in places like New York and Washington, DC, and were essentially chosen families of people who were LGBTQIA+. The concept has since been adopted with drag houses or drag families, which is where we get terms like "drag mother" or "drag child." It often/sometimes defines a queen's drag style, but mainly they're just a chosen family of people involved in the drag world. To put it in *Drag Race* context, Coco Montrese is Kahanna Montrese's drag mother and they are from the house of Montrese. Same for Crystal Methyd and Daya Betty; Alexis Mateo and Vanessa Vanjie Mateo; Sasha Colby and Kerri Colby; Tamisha Iman and LaLa Ri; and so on. Although that last one is a little contentious. A bit off topic but good information to have.

"We have this legendary queen here, Crystal Towers, who tried inducting me into her house, and I really didn't like it. And it's not on them. Her, and all of her daughters, and all of the family, were really sweet and cool. But what I didn't like about it was they reminded me so much of my actual family. And I was like, 'My family caused me so much fucking stress and anxiety, and now I'm a free gay adult, and yes, I do want to learn about this world, but I don't want to have to be answering to a mother. I don't want to get in a fight with any more sisters.'"

So, Yvie did their own thing, remaining an independent, which was a tactic that worked well for them. "After I won Ultimate Queen, it was like this springboard to try and refine everything else about my drag that I never even knew I could. I was finally past the stage of baby queen where you're like, 'How do I learn how to block my eyebrows and paint an illusion?' I was at this place where I was like, 'You know what, I'm going to be blue today, I'm going to be the blue queen. I'm going to be the queen who has her highlights where contours go, and contours where highlights go. I'm going to be the queen who has Cheerios glued on her face.' And it gave me so much freedom of expression."

Yvie has always described themself as a "conceptual" queen, which stems from the early days of their drag, but that too has been an evolution. "At that time, after I had mastered baby drag and started branching out more radically, I was partially conceptual because I think I was trying to disassociate from being human at all. Since I could be a boy or I could be a girl, what is next? What's more? And I fell in love with taking my old artistry and putting it into my new artistry. Having these alien creatures, or gorgeous women, or just strange materials used for outfits or makeup. And so that's where my birth of conceptualism came from: wanting to push the envelopes of what self-expression could be, because male and female still didn't feel right."

For an example of Yvie's concepts, we can look to their "gum outfit," which is exactly what it sounds like. "This came from one of the weeks in the Ultimate Queen competition that they had every year: an ABC challenge, or the Anything But Clothes challenge, where you have to wear or make an outfit out of anything but clothes. So, I was like, 'You know what would be funny for an ABC challenge? Is to wear some ABC (Already Been Chewed) gum.' My friends got together for a week, just chewing gum, putting it in the microwave to reheat it and make it malleable, attaching it onto a tutu, attaching it onto my hair. It was pretty sticky. Our house was disgusting. The outfit didn't get me anything because I didn't win the challenge that week. I'm proud of it though."

An outfit made entirely of gum is not something you see on most drag queens. It's that type of creativity and way-out-of-the-box thinking that speaks to Yvie's imagination and uniqueness, in all the best ways. Sure, they could have bought things off the rack, or learned to sew elaborate gowns. But making an outfit out of gum that was chewed by their friends? That's conceptual. That's creative. That's avant-garde. But it didn't stop there. Enter the "cigarette dress."

Yvie was working at Tracks (the Denver gay bar) and lived a block away with a bunch of other members of the community. Their house was the party house. Every weekend, and even throughout the week, there would be random parties with all sorts of people wandering in and out. And all those people would smoke in the house, and leave their cigarette butts everywhere, which was sort of okay because it wasn't exactly a palace. But Yvie saw something in those butts. They saw an outfit.

"Another drag queen had turned me on to the French electronic music producer Vitalic, and they have this song called 'Sweet Cigarette.' I was like, 'Oh, this is so clubby, and dark, and gross. And what if I just did a whole performance for my show outside in the alley out back, smoking cigarettes as a giant cigarette?' So I collected all the cigarettes from, I think, only two parties. I covered a Goodwill dress with all the cigarettes, and I still have it. I have to keep it in multiple bags, though, because she's a lot."

Over the years, Yvie's concepts have mellowed to some extent. "Now all these years later, I feel like I've come to terms with my own gender identity and how I choose to express on any given day. And I don't feel as othered from the world in the same ways that I used to. So I'm not trying to push my otherness, at least visually, in the same ways that I used to. Now a lot more of my concepts come from sociological elements. Because when you're doing drag as much as I do, you have to pack things that you can perform multiple nights in, multiple shows, multiple numbers. And so, where my drag before had really focused on creating one big visual impact, I now had to freak people out while still doing drag that was accessible. So I started womanizing, if you want to call it that—going back to painting, and just being and expressing just like a drag queen, like a girl, like another woman, another person on the planet. It was fun. I wish my brain still could work like it used to, but it's a little different when you're planning for six shows a week versus one show a month."

Today, Yvie's drag is less cigarette butts and more a blending of off-the-rack and incredible creativity. "Buying nice outfits has always been a part of my drag because I like seeing nice clothes and being like, 'Wow, I deserve that.' And sometimes you really don't have to make all that much of a change. There's always been some off-the-rack with me. But what I've always enjoyed more is when I can find something off-the-rack and either alter it, or pair it with other things that I've made. It's still a lot of balance. I buy a lot of off-the-rack, I buy things from designers, but I also make and remake a lot of my own shit still, whenever I can. Having a creative hand in my outfits is important for my overall identity."

Not surprisingly, Yvie's conceptuality extended beyond their outfits to their performances. "I was working at Tracks and had somehow bullied the manager into letting me have my own show on Thursdays called 'The Odd Hour,' specifically to be this one-of-a-kind spectacle where three times a night, in the middle of the club, twelve or thirteen clock chimes would happen and then on the screens we would project a live videographer somewhere in the club capturing a performer doing a strange-ass performance. It was this all-immersive experience where I wanted people to dress up and dress out. Be club kids and just know that sometime in the night you might be trying to get a drink, but some bitch is going to do a weird bloody ritual on a bar. It was the birth of queer spaces in Denver. It was the actual first queer event. And from there it just took off."

Yvie aspired to create spaces for queer people to be themselves, but also to make people feel uncomfortable. For Yvie, making people feel uncomfortable is about recognizing that the world is full of silly and unnecessary social constructs. Yvie liked challenging people's understanding of why things are the way they are. They want people to enjoy themselves, but they also want people to get a little uncomfortable, with the objective of seeing things differently.

"In the early days I would do anything to get a reaction. It's the same thing with a stand-up comedian. They need you to have a certain level of discomfort to make you laugh at some point. So you go everywhere: You talk about race, you talk about gender, you give visual shock. Eating crickets, doing death-defying stunts, looking like I'm about to fall and kill myself in the middle of a packed nightclub, twirling fire, taking a bath in a giant tub of cereal. I did it very, very intentionally, including intentional Blackface. And that's something that I still think people would be angry about today if they look far enough back. But I was having so much debate at the time about what it meant to be Black, and how Black queens should and shouldn't act, and what is and isn't the truth. I did it in part to shock but in part to create a conversation. Back then I would do literally anything to shock people that, for the most part, wasn't fucked up."

That desire to shock remains today. Yvie continues to be provocative and do things that challenge people. "One of my recent favorite numbers is just a drag queen mix, being sexy, taking off my clothes a little bit. But the final reveal is me taking off my panties to what looks like my giant erect dick swinging around. And it freaks people out because they can't believe that somebody this famous would just get on stage and take out their dick and let it swing around the world. I'm sure it makes some people happy, too. But I know it makes a lot of people uncomfortable to have to challenge the idea that this drag persona they admire is also still a sexual human being."

For Yvie, drag was a calling, starting with the early days of *Drag Race* airing, long before Ru girls were going on international tours and appearing in commercials with Cardi B. Historically, drag queens performed in gay bars, often working for tips and a bar tab. For the queens appearing on early seasons of *Drag Race*, not much changed beyond having name recognition and getting to perform in bars and at Pride festivals across the United States. As the show has become more and more popular, the opportunities for contestants have improved. "When I started doing drag, it was without the real glamour of it all. Of course, there's the glamour of being on TV and shit. But the glamour for me, that called me to drag, was the way that people were going to see me, the way that my art would be digested. That I would have a face in the community that would make it okay and not matter that all of my White twinky friends were all fucking everyone and everything that lived, but I couldn't get laid to save my life. Even if it didn't make all of those other things go away, it made it okay because I had purpose. I was good at it. It feels so good to know that you're good at something, even if other people don't feel that way. It gave me everything in one place. Before, it felt like I had to choose an art form even in my adult life. I'd be working on some paintings for a while, and then I'd go do a theater production. Drag was the one place where it was everything all in one. What was terrifying about it was that it was going to change my identity to only being a drag queen."

From those early days of a red wig and a Ross dress, Yvie continued to evolve and define themselves. They continued to build up their reputation in Denver, which led to being invited to perform in other cities. They persisted at challenging people with their art. They kept working at honing their craft to the point where they were ready to take on the world.

YVIE'S TOP 5 DRUGS

1. Weed. She's good for every situation even if it makes me a lil' forgetful.

2. Mushrooms. They're almost spiritual for me so it's weird to include them on a list of "drugs."

3. Molly. Who doesn't like feeling good and dancing?

4. Pot. She's good for every situation even if it makes me a lil' forgetful.

5. Drag. Only just beating out alcohol and cocaine, but to be fair you can get your fill of those if you do enough drag.

CHAPTER 4

CALIFORNIA DREAMING: THE DRAGOLYMPICS

RuPaul's Drag Race has been called the Olympics of Drag—by RuPaul, of course. And it sort of is. But it sort of isn't.

The Olympics are a competition where the only thing that matters is your ability in your respective sport. When Tom Daley was selected to represent the UK at the 2012 Olympics in London, the British Olympic Association likely wasn't terribly concerned about his social media following or how the fans might respond to him during the broadcast. They cared about his ability to land a dive with perfect form.

RuPaul's Drag Race is a reality television show that uses a drag contest as its main storyline. The mission of the show is not to give out the gold medal to the world's best—or even America's best—drag queen. It's to make a television show about a contest to find America's next drag superstar. It's a reality television show first, and a competition second. That is an important distinction that will impact Yvie's experience with the show.

Before we get to that, we need to talk about why Yvie wanted to be on the show and their journey to becoming a Ru girl. "I mean, not that it was the only goal for me when I started doing drag, but that kind of exposure, that kind of platform to have people see my art, is pretty enticing. I wasn't looking for fame and fortune. It was a chance to actually be important for the things that I've always really valued about myself, that I didn't feel like the world always valued about me. So that was my main push when I thought about auditioning; it was just a matter of time. When I started doing drag, I was eighteen and the show has a twenty-one age limit. So I thought I'd take those three years to learn about drag, do drag, get better at drag. And in those three years I went from Avon LaRue to Avon Eve to Yvie Oddly. They were important years in my development and set me on course for eventually getting on the show a few years later. During that buildup I got to see not only how my numbers would play out with live audiences, but to see how the culture works. You get to see what it's like to try and book a show, or be in a show, or interact with people at the bar, because you're always selling yourself. In the years before I got on *Drag Race*, I was constantly learning, growing, and trying to expand: expand my world and expand my influence as much as I could. My first audition was when I was twenty-one because it was the first year I could, but also because it was the first year that I felt I was bigger than Denver. I'm pretty sure that year, or close to it, I'd traveled out of state for the first time to do drag and I thought, 'Oh, not only am I good here, but I'm also good in Arkansas and New Mexico.'" For a point of reference, Yvie turned twenty-one in August 2014, and then won Track's Ultimate Queen in July 2015.

Even as Yvie was performing in bars outside of their home city, they were still a long way from drag superstardom, let alone being able to make a living in drag. "You can be the best of the best in your city, and it still won't mean a lot. In Denver there was a lot of talk too about how RuPaul secretly hated Denver for some reason. It always sounded like bullshit to me. But as a queen trying to make your name bigger, and you're not in Chicago, and you're not in New York, and you're not in LA, you already feel like you're at a disadvantage because we're never going to have thousands of followers, which is what that world was like at that moment. But it was kind of the beginning of that transition from having Facebook friends to, 'Oh no, bitch, you need to have Instagram followers if you want the opportunity to perform in another state, or maybe make a shitty drag queen song.'"

So, with that goal in mind, Yvie set out to get cast on *RuPaul's Drag Race.*

AUDITION TAPE 1: SEASON 9 WINNER: SASHA VELOUR

By this point, the show had eight seasons in the can—which is what they say in the "biz"—so people had developed an understanding

@LiamDrawsDrag

of what a good audition tape looked like, but that didn't make it any easier. It's a challenging process to make an audition tape that sums up exactly who you are and what you could bring to the show. World of Wonder, the show's production company, receives thousands of audition tapes every season, and the challenge for a contestant is to stand out from the crowd.

"The first audition tape was really nerve wracking, and really uncomfortable. There's this mindset that you can go into auditions, or job interviews, holding these nerves and not feeling like you deserve that position. Being like, 'Oh my God, I'm going to have to beg and show them all my best parts if I want them to hire me, if I want to work here, if I want the opportunity.' And that really showed in my first audition. Even as I was having my friends help me edit it, I wasn't proud of it. It felt painful to show my friends, and it felt painful to sit through twenty minutes of me being like, 'I'm Yvie Oddly, and I'm from Denver. And of course, I'm America's next drag superstar because I'm a weirdo.' And then it'd go to clips of me, because they ask you for fucking everything. They ask for Snatch Game, an acting scene, and basically anytime it came to a performance where I knew the camera was on me, I got choked up, and nervous, and just inauthentic. It was painful to watch. But then there's still the parts of me that I was really proud of. They ask you to make a dress out of paper; that dress was fucking gorgeous."

Ultimately, Yvie wasn't successful in their application. "Even though I believe I was ready as a drag artist, there's another thing that is so hard to factor in when you're thinking about going on *Drag Race*, and that's being ready as, if not a television personality, then an interesting, actual, natural portrayal of who you are, of just an interesting character. And I was treating it like a job interview, and I was like, 'I got my name Yvie Oddly because I'm even odder than everybody else. I like to perform to raunchy rap music because it's fun.' Just question-answer, instead of shooting the shit, letting myself ramble, telling outrageous stories. I wasn't ready for the reality TV aspect of *Drag Race* in the slightest. I just had a friend videotape some of my performances one night. And I figured, 'Yup, that was good, that was me. They can see all of my flips, they can see all of my passion, they can see my ingenuity.' But for the rest of it? I wasn't me. Not that I wasn't Yvie, it's just that it didn't connect in the video; it didn't connect to who I was. I was terrified to go all the way. I was just another nervous twink wanting to get on *Drag Race*."

AUDITION TAPE 2: SEASON 10 WINNER: AQUARIA

Another year passed, and Yvie took another kick at the can. But what changed from the previous year? "The second tape was better because at least I was used to the challenges that they were asking of me. The first year, I literally did the Snatch Game last-minute, like, in the last second of filming I threw on two different wigs. In the second year I was like, 'Okay, I'm going to go in with characters and ideas beforehand, and actually tackle all of the challenges that they give me instead of being like, yeah, here it is. This is the one I actually like.' So, in that aspect, it was better. And my interviews were a little more authentic. But I think I also have this habit of being too wordy, too deep, and too lengthy for reality TV. I speak in a train of thought. You can hear my sentences forming as I'm speaking. My brain can move fast, but my body and my words are not at that same speed. So, the second year I was better in some ways. But I think my downfall was that I was still so passionate about getting on, that too much of the 'twink who wants to be on *Drag Race*' shone through in my interviews, by me being like, 'I'm so passionate about being a weirdo because I'm not represented in the culture here. And I never get to see myself on TV.'"

What no one tells you, when you're submitting an audition tape for a show like *Drag Race,* is the pain of the waiting game you have to endure. You don't submit your tape and receive a message back with a thumbs-up or -down emoji. You click send and then wait months before you hear anything, if you hear anything at all. "I think the first year I might not have even gotten a generic email telling me I didn't get in. I just had to assume I didn't get on. But the second year, after waiting for months thinking, 'Maybe today is the day that I'll hear something about that thing I did that has been in the back of my mind,' I finally got that email that said something like, 'Hey, kitty girl, it's not your year but we appreciate your submission. Try again in the future. Stay fierce, diva.'"

With the first audition tape, not hearing anything may have been more of a blessing. With the second audition tape, getting what may have come across as a generic "thank you for applying" letter was more of a gut punch. "It deflates your bubble. You see it every year in the wave of girls. Especially now that people are so much more vocal about not getting on and shit. It deflates your bubble because we, as drag artists, know that we have so much to give. And I think even before the world of the money and fame that comes with *Drag Race*, it was just a chance to be seen and to have people be like, 'Yes, Miss Sasha Winzington Delicatrosse the third, from Ohio, you are that bitch. Those girls in your local scene who talked shit about you, and didn't book you in that show, they don't know what's up. You're going to get on *Drag Race* and show them.'

"I was frustrated year after year, seeing them cast everybody and seeing closeness to my representation but never seeing myself there. And being like, 'I believe you guys won't put me on, but you'll put on a skinny White hoe who can't do anything but walk the runway in the expensive clothes that her friends made her.' I know that sounds like I'm digging at a specific queen. But trust me, I've worked with all of them, and I love them, and I respect them, and it's so much deeper than that. It's just, as a young hungry viewer, as somebody who feels like the world is always pushing you to the side or ignoring you, or looking right through you, it was frustrating to never feel like I was going to have a shot."

AUDITION TAPE 3: SEASON 11 WINNER: WELL, YOU KNOW

Something changed with Yvie and their approach between the tape for season 10 and the tape they submitted for what would be their season. Yvie took an entirely different approach to creating their audition tape. Rather than following the same format

Marina Sputnik @ @sputnik_blindheart

they had previously followed, they approached the audition like it was a short film. And they did it all by themself.

"For the first time, I decided not to put this in anyone else's hands. I taught myself how to edit videos specifically to make this vision that I had. It was the full package, and I mean bigger than even *RuPaul's Drag Race*. If I had never said RuPaul once in that video, it was still the full package of everything I was—what I wanted to mean and did mean to the world in that moment. I honestly feel like my audition video is the reason I won, because it was the artist statement that really stuck with them. And it stuck with the fans, who ultimately decide the winner. That audition tape had a clear statement: 'Yes, I'm not the best. I'm not the cleanest. I'm not the prettiest. Not always going to do the most predictable shit, but I'm so passionate about following these weird artistic dreams, and just doing it honestly.'"

What Yvie's talking about is authenticity. It's what RuPaul and Michelle (Visage, obviously) talk about on the show all the time. It's about showing the world who you are, not who you think the world wants to see. It may seem trite—we hear Ru say it every season—but there's truth in those words. The most successful artists are the ones who are willing to be vulnerable and let the world see exactly who they are, warts and all. It's through that vulnerability that fans of the show fall in love with the queen and want to see them succeed. Not every fan is going to love every queen, but the ones who let down their guard the most, and let people see their truth, are the ones who are going to reach the biggest audience. Yet, that is easier said than done. "That's really the key to doing anything on the show. But that's the hardest thing to develop as a skill, truly. Especially when something's so scary and it's your first time. Your survival instinct of panic takes over instead of being like, 'I am capable. And if I was going to do this challenge, this is how I would do it. If I was going to walk this runway, this is how I would walk it.'"

Yet, some people didn't think Yvie had it in her to make it to *Drag Race*. "In Colorado, Jessica L'Whor—who is the same drag age as me and came up and got big in the scene at the same time as me—was this perfect package for *Drag Race*. She had already made YouTube videos, and she ran basically every single show here. She read to children and was good at talking on camera. And she was White, so while I really did come up in this gritty way in the scene, begging people to give me a chance, doing all these competitions, I had this peer who was a shining example of how, even in a queer community, being White and (at least at the time) identifying as a cis male was really helpful for getting you in places. I won't forget the year that I finally got on, I had had some stupid conversation with some twink at a bar, drunk, late at night. And he was like, 'Yeah, this is going to be the year that Jessica gets on. She's already done two tapes before. And I love you, girl, but this is her year and I think you just need more time.' That was one of the fires that made me make such a fierce audition tape that year."

It's important to know who Yvie submitted for their Snatch Game. Yes, Snatch Game. In their audition tape, Yvie had to submit three characters, which included Whoopi Goldberg, Tiffany Haddish, and their best friend Teena. "I did a made-up interpretation of my best friend, because I think she's one of the craziest fucking characters I have met in my life."

A week after submitting their video, Yvie got an email from World of Wonder: "Hey, do you have any other Snatch Game characters? Teena was hilarious but that wouldn't work." That's when Yvie knew they had a chance of getting cast. "I scream, I panic, I freak out, I tell my roommate, I tell my videographer friend, I pee myself a little bit, I pee myself a lot. I submit one more character, it might have been Cardi B or something. Or maybe Tim Gunn. I don't know."

So, Yvie submitted their second Snatch Game tape of Cardi B or Tim Gunn—who are very easy to confuse—and then went back to living their life. They continued doing shows and working on their craft, but this time they had a different feeling because they had a strong suspicion that they had made it on.

"I was still doing bigger and bigger things with my drag career in Denver. I'd performed at Red Rocks Park and Amphitheatre in Morrison, Colorado. I had my own show up and running. I was judging Ultimate Queen. All of these things to distract myself from the fact that I felt like this could be my time for *Drag Race*. And then I got a call. It wasn't the 'You got on' call. But this is the first time I'd spoken to anyone from World of Wonder [WOW], and I still don't remember who the fuck I talked to because I was so excited."

While it wasn't a confirmation of being cast, it was the next step, and this was the first time Yvie started to believe it was really going to happen. It was the first tangible contact Yvie had with the show. The WOW producer swore Yvie to secrecy but scheduled them for a psychological evaluation, which every queen has to go through before getting on.

A few weeks later Yvie had another call with the WOW producer to start to get a better sense of who Yvie is, in real (unedited) time. "I think they just wanted to see how much of my story I would be willing to give them. Because we had an hour-long conversation, and in that hour I'm like, 'Yeah, I'm a weirdo . . . child abuse . . . and also, I like alien stuff . . . and also, I've always felt ostracized sexually for this, which is why I became a drag queen.'"

And that was it. A few weeks later, on a random rainy day, Yvie got the call from the WOW producer to let them know Yvie would be part of the cast of *RuPaul's Drag Race* season 11. Yvie screamed with joy at finally achieving that goal. They had spent six years honing their craft and developing their drag with the objective of getting on the world's biggest drag platform, and they were finally there. The most important part of that moment was that Yvie felt seen. They felt like their drag had been recognized as valid, and worthy of being shown to the world. That day was a pinnacle moment in their career—the moment that would see Yvie become a global drag superstar . . . provided they could survive what came next.

YVIE'S TOP 5
SONGS TO FUCK TO

1. "Sex With Me" Rihanna

2. "12.38" Childish Gambino

3. "Pocky Boy" Yeule

4. "Notion" Tash Sultana

5. "New Person, Same Old Mistakes" Tame Impala

CHAPTER 5

THE MAIN EVENT: REFLECTIONS FROM SEASON 11 OF *RUPAUL'S DRAG RACE*

T wo and a half weeks. That's how long Yvie had to prepare. From that call from an unknown World of Wonder producer on that rainy day, to getting on a plane to fly to Los Angeles to film season 11 of *RuPaul's Drag Race*, Yvie had a total of two and a half weeks to prepare. Whether or not that is enough time—and whether it aligns with other similar reality television shows—is anyone's guess. One thing is certain: It threw Yvie into a state of sheer panic. "They give you a list with ten possible runways, and vague characters you'll need for challenges. For example, 'orange and fringe' runway, and 'your eleganza' runway, obviously, and your 'what really is your drag' runway, and a 'family resemblance' runway. And then they give you characters like a hooker, an old lady, a good old Southern girl. And those were easy for me because at this point my roommate Morgan and I had started secretly, very stealthily, looping in other people. Because he was like, 'You literally can't do this alone. And no offense, but your drag is ugly. Your drag is ugly and busted. And you have really good ideas, but they will look so, so ugly as they are, on the mainstage. So, you need to buy everything or make everything from scratch.'"

With that, Yvie realized they needed help to ensure they could get everything together for the show, particularly securing some investment dollars, all of which had to be done in secret because contestants swear on pain of death that they won't tell anyone they've been cast. "I decided to secretly loop in my boss at Tracks. They gave me time off from work, and seven thousand dollars, which I'd never had in my life. And they gave me their support as long as I agreed to come do some shows for them in the future, and of course I said, 'I'm a Ru girl now, of course I'll do shows for you.' But I was still working day shifts for them because they weren't just going to pay me seven thousand dollars for nothing. So I would do the daytime bar-stocking shift. I'd just sit there at the nightclub in the daytime waiting for food and liquor trucks to deliver their orders. And in the meantime, be sewing and gluing. Not actually sewing, just gluing, gluing, gluing, and freaking out, and sketching, and gluing. My roommate had started looping in other close friends of mine to work shit out. So, there was always three or four people at our house just cutting shit, making shit."

One thing that is very common in unscripted television is that things are pretty fluid, right up until filming, and even during the shoot. There are a huge number of moving pieces in the background that the contestants don't see, and as the show starts to take shape, with writers finalizing episodes, changes can and do occur. That can be a challenge for some competitors because they have to adapt as things change. "The hard part of getting ready was that they never send you a complete list. A week after they gave me the first list, they sent an updated list and they're like, 'And actually, we want these things in addition.'"

Yvie carefully called on people they could trust to help them put together their wardrobe, while still keeping Yvie's appearance on the show top secret. "I reached out to basically every connection I had that I was close with in Denver, from all parts of my life. I talked to this fashion designer that I once walked in a runway for. I talked to a kid I went to high school with who became a fashion designer. I talked to the drag queens who judged me in the competition, like Nina Flowers, and borrowed things from them. And we did all of this at first in my living room, and then we realized we needed more space and moved it to a friend's garage, which was perfect because we could just stay there all day and all night chain smoking, drinking coffee, inhaling Red Bull, and making shit. And as prepared as you can try and be, and as much stuff as you can try and do in advance, literally up until the vans came to pick me up in the morning, I was stuffing shit in my suitcases: the last tights here, and a wig there, and a shoe here. And wondering 'Is this fifty pounds? Oh fuck.'"

Let's take a breath and recap, because that was a lot of information covering a short period of time. Yvie had two and a half weeks to prepare for the biggest opportunity of their life to date. By their own admission, Yvie's drag wasn't really television ready at that point in their career. The tutu made of chewed gum and the cigarette dress were not going to read well on the mainstage. So, Yvie wasn't really able to pull something from their closet that would potentially fit the brief, unlike some of the other queens. Yvie simply didn't have an extensive wardrobe that would not only fit the brief of each challenge but would also scream "superstar" to RuPaul and the panel of judges. That meant they had to start from scratch on much of their wardrobe, leaving them feeling like they were starting at a disadvantage compared to the other queens.

Before we get back to Yvie, some people might not understand what the "pageant scene" is, and it's very relevant to the story. Drag pageants are just like they sound—a beauty pageant, like Miss America. But instead of the contestants being pretty young women from rural America, they're drag performers . . . from rural America. There are bar competitions, city competitions, state competitions, and national competitions. The most famous pageants are the likes of Miss Continental and Miss Continental Plus, Miss Gay America, Miss Gay USofA, and Entertainer of the Year—which many Ru girls have won, including season 11's Brooke Lynn Hytes, A'keria C. Davenport, and Nina West. Drag pageants are a way for queens to polish their act, garner a following, and in turn, accumulate a lot of outfits that can be recycled later. Like when you're cast on *RuPaul's Drag Race*.

Season 11 happened to have a significant number of "pageant queens," which is not a bad thing as much as it is a fact. Pageant queens tend to have a particular style and aesthetic, and that pageant experience can be a benefit to a *Drag Race* contestant. "There is an advantage if you already have things in your closet," Yvie explains. "A lot of girls I competed with came from the pageant world. And if the category was vague enough, they had things to fit. So, it felt like a big disadvantage when I had spent the most money I had ever had in my life and worked the hardest I ever had in my life on these concepts. Specifically, with the idea of standing out and telling my story and giving my point of view in a way that I don't get to do in Denver."

"When you have to do the best drag of your life, and you only get one night, and one look, and one runway, you're going to go as hard as possible. So, it was weird going in, spending my measly seven thousand dollars, and then getting there and just being blinded by rhinestones. And even if the girls weren't necessarily pageant queens, I think it may have just been the aesthetic of the time. But everybody, for the most part, was a blinged out, big expensive jewelry, big expensive hair, big expensive gowns kinda queen. Or they rented big expensive designer items and shit. And I was thinking, 'I am so out of my league.' I used more stones than I've ever stoned in my drag career, and it still looked like my dress may have had a bad case of pimples."

Spending seven thousand dollars might not seem measly, but it's important to contextualize the range of what contestants have spent in preparation for appearing on the show. Trixie Mattel said they spent six hundred dollars preparing for their appearance on season 7. Gottmik, who appeared on season 13, has said they spent twenty thousand dollars. Icesis Couture, winner of *Canada's Drag Race* season 2, reportedly spent seventy thousand dollars in planning for their appearance on *Canada's Drag Race: Canada vs. the World.* Seven thousand dollars is not a small amount of money, particularly when you borrow it, but it's also not anywhere near as much as some others have invested.

Yvie flew to Los Angeles exhausted, stressed, and unsure of themself. Their dream was coming true, but were they ready for it? "They meet you at the airport and they kidnap you. Which is only halfway a joke." Secrecy in the competition is critically important. World of Wonder works very hard to ensure the contestants are separated until they walk into the Werk Room. They want that element of surprise to be captured on camera, particularly when the queens know one another. Like when Coco Montrese walked into the Werk Room on season 5 and the camera cut to Alyssa Edwards and the look that screamed "gooped!" That type of reaction cannot be faked.

"I can't remember if I'm fabricating this," Yvie recalls, "but I definitely do remember my vision being obscured as we drove to the hotel, and them taking my phone literally the second they got me from the airport. And then before I even got in the hotel room, they took my luggage away and then brought it to the hotel room to search. I don't remember how long I had in the hotel room. I think it was only a day or so. But you have a little bit of time to mentally prepare yourself for the fact that you're going to be going into *Drag Race*. Of course, the night before, I did not sleep a wink. Especially because they don't let you have the things to make it easy to go to bed. So, while you're sitting there stressing about making the best first impression on the biggest day of your life, you can't watch some porn and jack off and go to bed. There's no glass of wine to help you. There's no pot, which is a big, big thing for me. It's just such a wild process from the jump. It's like going from having this concept of *Drag Race* to entering full lockdown to prepare for the Hunger Games." Yvie's referring to something that many *Drag Race* contestants have talked about: the *perception* of *Drag Race*, and the *reality* of *Drag Race*. You may have an idea of what the experience is going to be, but the reality may be quite different, specifically, a lot more intense.

One sleepless, never-ending night later, Yvie started to get ready for the big entrance. "At like four or five in the morning I started painting my face and stressing about the little things and stressing about hair and jewelry. And then they grab you, and you're isolated some more. I remember they took me to the studio and put me in a room by myself. This is all just so that the queens don't know who's there with them. But they put me in some office in my little skimpy dress all alone. I don't remember how long I was there; it could have been multiple hours. But I do know that it was long enough for me to fall asleep and take a nap."

Beyond sleeping, the isolation gave Yvie time to reflect . . . which was the last thing they needed in that moment. "It's such a terrifying experience. From the isolation to the knowing that this is about to be a big moment. It's terrifying and overwhelming, and it's the same heart-in-my-throat feeling I've gotten every time I had an audition or a job interview."

Then came the moment of truth. Yvie walked into the Werk Room. They wore an emerald green floor-length sleeveless dress with a hem of green feathers, matching elbow-length opera gloves, and an obscene amount of gold chains. They wore a black bob wig that they had styled with an extreme widow's peak that came down to their eyes. To finish the look, there was a green toy car attached to a black boa driving ahead of them. They confidently hit their mark and uttered their first *Drag Race* catchphrase, "Move over, ladies, this race just took an odd turn." They had arrived.

Episode 1: "Whatcha Unpackin?"

Fourteen new queens and one returning queen (Vanessa Vanjie Mateo) enter the Werk Room. Yvie is the ninth to enter, wearing a floor-length emerald green dress with a boa attached to the hem, which is attached to a toy car that Yvie is controlling. Yvie's entrance line is, "Move over, ladies, this race just took an odd turn." For the mini-challenge, each contestant is paired with another Ru girl from a previous season for a photo shoot. Yvie is paired with Alaska. For the maxi-challenge, the queens create a look using material belonging to former *Drag Race* competitors. New crew member "Barry Johnson, aka BJ" enters the Werk Room and Silky is the first one to figure out BJ is actually guest judge Miley Cyrus. The queens lose their shit and Silky runs around the Werk Room with Miley on her back. On the mainstage, Brooke Lynn Hytes wins the challenge, Yvie is safe, and Kahanna Montrese and Soju are in the bottom. They lip-sync to "The Best of Both Worlds" by Hannah Montana (another disguise for Miley). Soju is sent home.

"I think no matter what age you are, going from such a dramatically real-life experience to a surreal reality TV experience, I'm honestly surprised that you don't see the nerves showing in more girls' faces when we all walk in. I can still see it in mine. But it's just so much to take in, and the strange part about all of it is you're kind of waiting for a 'ready, set, go.' And then an explanation of how the race is going to work. But you're just kind of thrown into every situation, where you hold on by the seat of your pants." Yvie was expecting some instruction from producers on how things were going to play out, but that's not how reality television operates. The producers want the contestants' reactions to be genuine, so they keep them on their toes, and keep explanations to a minimum. It's that type of planned chaos that has won *Drag Race* countless awards, including over one hundred Primetime Emmy nominations to date. It's television gold.

Yvie definitely got a reaction from the other queens. Vanjie's comment on camera was, "Oh girl, the circus is in town, Mary," and Honey said, "So she's House Slytherin," referring to one of the student residences in the Harry Potter series. In confessional, Honey exclaimed, "I'm really confused why Hot Wheels needs to make an appearance on *RuPaul's Drag Race*."

Silky's first impression was relatively similar. "Yvie wasn't my type of drag, to be honest. I just remember I said, 'Who is this booger queen walking in here in this green?' That's all I can remember. Like, 'Look at this booger queen.' I was like, 'Uh,' with chicken feathers, and green, and this little . . . I think it was a little car or something. I just remember her having the little thing in her hand. And I was just like, 'Oh my God, look at this little queen.'"

Not everyone felt the same. Brooke Lynn Hytes's thoughts differed from some of the other competitors': "My first impression of Yvie was I knew immediately, just by looking at her and then looking around the room, that she was going to be in the competition for a long time."

Yvie's entrance look was, as anticipated, conceptual, and there was a lot of thought behind it. The dress and jewelry were on loan from Nina Flowers, but the concept was all Yvie. As they explain it, "I've always, always, wanted to do a look where it looks like you're walking out face forward. And then you turn around and it's actually your face, like a two-faced person, I always wanted to do that. So that's where this came from, this idea of, 'Okay, so how could I have the back of me showing first?' And then my roommate said, 'Well, what if you attached a little car to it or something?' And then the idea completely devolved from being the backward space thing, which I've played with a few times, to being like, "You know what, I'm just going to drive this stupid little remote-control car, and it's going to be very Yzma from *The Emperor's New Groove*, what with her little gadgets and gizmos she's always fucking with, especially with Nina Flowers's dress and jewelry. And that morning, when I

Reed Perry (she/her) 📷 *@dropdeadbeautie*

woke up to do my makeup, I just wanted to make sure that people knew I wasn't there to be pretty. So, I spiked that one big spike of hair down in the center, I pinned the necklace in, and then I just painted the biggest, greenest, most snakelike eyes I could. Just to show people I'm not coming in a lady."

Looking across the cast, Yvie stood out, but maybe not in a way they wanted to. Season 11's cast was made up of two distinct groups: pageant queens and social media queens. The pageant queens were A'keria, Brooke Lynn, Honey, Kahanna, Mercedes, Nina, Ra'Jah, Scarlet, Silky, and Vanjie—that's ten of fifteen queens. The social media queens—the ones whose experience prior to *Drag Race* was primarily (although not exclusively) on social media—were Soju, Ariel, and Plastique. That left Shuga Cain (who had only been doing drag professionally for about a year before being cast) and Yvie. It was those groupings that assured Yvie they were *not* going to be a "filler queen"—a contestant who is thought to be unlikely to go very far in the competition, because someone has to go home each episode. "That's the strange thing, going into the whole experience and knowing how broke I was, and how little I knew about how this world worked; I still felt like I wasn't going to be a filler queen, which is why after the last girl had walked in the door, I felt a little disappointed with my season. And I know it sounds like the shadiest thing that you can say about a bunch of girls that you shared an experience with and got to know deeply. But it's just how I felt when I looked around and I was like, 'Well, I guess we're the Blackest season, so that's cool for us.' But the fact was, there was so much of one specific type of drag representation." In case you don't have it memorized, there were seven Black, two Asian, two LatinX, and four White contestants.

Yvie's perspective at the time may seem a bit harsh but that's not the intention. Yvie looked across the cast of season 11 and didn't see a lot of uniqueness in the style of drag that the queens were bringing. There weren't any other "alternative" queens like Nina Bo'nina Brown (season 9) or Jimbo (*All Stars*, season 8). But arguably there was still a lot of diversity within the cast. Mercedes was the first Muslim queen on the show. Plastique was the first and only Vietnamese queen to enter the Werk Room. Brooke Lynn was the first Canadian. Kahanna had a Las Vegas showgirl thing going on. Soju was only the second Korean queen to be on the show, and the first to share with the world about their exploding cyst. #overshare. While there was a lot of similarity in style of drag of the season 11 cast, there was variety within the cast. Yvie didn't think the cast was bad. Just that there wasn't a lot of diversity in the aesthetic.

Yvie wasn't alone. Brooke Lynn recognized it immediately, and felt it was what made Yvie bigger competition. As she explains, "Our season was very heavy on the pretty pageant queens, very that vein of pretty drag. It was very, very heavy on that. I think probably maybe more so than any season before, or since. And she really was the only weirdo we had in our entire cast. I'm just scanning through to think, and really, she was kind of in a league of her own in that way. I was like, 'There's no way she's going to go home early because she's going to bring a completely different perspective than everyone else, and I believe the show needs that.'"

Episode 2: "Good God Girl, Get Out"

For the mini-challenge of episode 2, the queens photo-bomb celebrity snapshots, with Brooke Lynn and Silky winning the challenge. For the maxi-challenge, the contestants perform in drag adaptations of the movies *Black Panther* (called "Why It Gotta Be Black, Panther?") and *Get Out* (called "Good God Girl, Get Out"). Yvie is part of Team Good God Girl, Get Out and delivers what can only be described as one of the most disturbing laughs in television history. On the runway, the category is What's Your Sign? with Yvie wearing their iconic silver and copper digital lion outfit, representing their astrological sign Leo. Scarlet and Yvie both win the challenge. Kahanna and Mercedes, in the bottom, lip-sync to "Work Bitch" by Britney Spears. Kahanna is sent packing.

What you see in the episodes is pretty much what actually occurs. There isn't much that happens off-camera. The queens aren't given time to process the experience, nor to socialize and build a rapport before they dive into the deep end. Again, this is reality television. The producers want to capture as much on camera as possible so they can use it to build the storylines. But bonds already existed, at least in theory. As Yvie puts it, "Within that first day I went from being so panicked about this whole experience, and how the beginning of it was going to feel, to thinking, 'Oh my God, it's going to be over immediately' because they gave us a challenge, and it was a 'Stay up all night and work on an outfit' challenge. So, it's now two nights of no sleep, manically hot-gluing shit with a bunch of people I feel so uncomfortable with, because I don't know them. And also, they're my competitors. What made it more terrifying is right from the start, there was a connection between all the pageant girls. All the girls who came from the pageant world, knew of the pageant world, or were related to the pageant world all immediately had something to bond about. And then there was a handful of social media superstars who all were like, 'Oh my God, we're just going to bond because we all know what it's like to be on Instagram, and we're so pretty,' and worried about that or whatever."

Yvie wasn't imagining that. As Silky confirms, "I knew, I think, four girls going into it. That was Vanjie, because of television. I knew A'keria because of pageants, Nina West because of pageants, and I worked with Brooke Lynn, and it was because of pageants."

That instant connection between others left Yvie feeling on the outside. As they explain, "From the start, they were talking about their pageant girl backgrounds, and who they were expecting to see here, and who they knew was going to be here already. And I felt like I was already at so much of a disadvantage. Looking around at their expensive costumes, watching them unpack these expensive wigs with all of this knowledge from *Drag Race* alumni. 'Detox let me borrow this,' and 'Oh, Alexis gave me her guy for that.' I'm competing against a literal fucking meme, Miss Vanjie, in the prime of Miss Vanjiedom." Yvie may not have thought they were a filler queen, but that didn't mean that they were feeling overly confident. The closeness between the other contestants left Yvie feeling excluded, regardless of whether it was deliberate or not.

The competition began immediately. Silky, who had won the mini-challenge on episode 1, assigned trunks from former contestants to each of the queens. They would have to use what was in the trunk to create the look for the mainstage. As Silky said in confessional, "We all deserve to be here. If you go home, you're going home on your own accord. So, I give everybody similar to what they're giving." Meaning, she assigned the trunk based on her impression of the queen, keeping in mind that Silky had spent all of an hour with the queens at that point. Alaska's trunk was wrapped in garbage bags and Silky felt that best aligned with Yvie. Shady? That's certainly how Yvie took it: "The fact that pretty much out of the gate, the girls, they weren't mean or anything, they weren't picking on me. But they made it clear that they saw me as a trash queen. Silky gave me Alaska's box because she knows that I can work with garbage, which is pretty strong out of the gate, having seen one look."

Silky saw it differently: "I didn't know Yvie. We met in a room for maybe an hour when everybody walked in, and then we never saw each other again until that moment. They were trying to make it seem like I was shading Plastique. I didn't shade Plastique, I didn't know her, I didn't know anyone. I was very fair to everybody. Everybody got something that was close to them. I didn't have any strategy. I didn't try to sabotage. Honey Davenport got Kennedy Davenport because I felt the family resemblance, you know? I gave myself Peppermint because I was the big Black girl. Thinking about it now, I would have done it completely different knowing everybody's personalities, but I still probably would have gave Yvie Alaska, because who else would she have gotten?"

We now have a new theme emerging for Yvie: imposter syndrome. Ru calls it the inner saboteur, but we're talking about the same thing: self-doubt. It's one thing when you're ruling the local bar scene, but it's an entirely different situation when you're walking the mainstage of the world's biggest drag reality television show. Doubt is natural. Doubt is expected. If you don't doubt yourself in a situation like that, one might question your grasp on reality. Or you're Sasha Belle. *Drag Race* superfans will get that joke. The rest of you can go back and watch the first two episodes of *Drag Race* season 7.

Yvie was not an exception to the rule. Doubt showed up for Yvie throughout the competition. They were terrified that they would be the first queen to go home. But when RuPaul announced them as safe, they were able to breathe again. "It was very overwhelming. And all of that anxiety just powered through until Ru said I was safe. I've never felt better in my life than that first week when RuPaul called me safe. I don't understand how people could be bitter at being safe in that first week. I don't care if I made the most gorgeous outfit, I just don't want you to crush my dream this early."

Lonely is the word Yvie uses to describe their time on *Drag Race*. As they explain it, "I pride myself on being very independent. But the cast dynamics, or the dynamic I had with the cast, was that most of us were not on good terms. And even if we were, it's not like anyone would ever have my back when I was popping off. It was just this weird sense of everybody trying just a little too hard, especially because everybody tried to be sisters, too, or at least they would say that they were. There was so much hypocrisy that I just never felt fully close to anyone. Day one, all of us Black girls got together and were like, 'Wow, there are more Black girls on this show than there have ever been before. Half of our cast is Black, we're here to represent. We have to stick with each other. And this is going to be so magical.' Bitch, our entire season was Black girls attacking Black girls. It was literally that way from the jump." Put together the feelings of loneliness and exclusion, and add in the imposter syndrome and insecurity, combined with everything we already know about Yvie's personality, and it starts to explain the behavior that we saw from Yvie: the shadiness, the arguments, the aggression, the fights. In retrospect, it's no wonder they acted the way they did.

Season 11 was arguably one of the more heated seasons, and often Yvie was at the center of the fire. More recent seasons of *Drag Race* have been defined as a sisterhood—at least that's what we see on camera. But not season 11, as Yvie shares: "Our season might most poignantly be defined by the drama between me and Silky. But it was everyone. I'm actually on really good terms with every single person now. There's not one girl from the cast who I have any ill will toward, who I believe has any real negative feelings toward me or whatever." At the time, however, there was tension between Yvie and Silky, Yvie and Ra'Jah, Yvie and Vanessa . . . and that's just what we saw on camera.

Some might suggest this is a "blame it on the edit" moment, where producers only showed viewers one side of the story. A lot of what we saw showed Yvie as a target of aggressive behavior. But there are two sides to every story. Silky explains the blowup that occurred on *Untucked*, during episode 3's Diva Worship challenge. "They always show it like Yvie was defending herself. In reality, Yvie would poke at us. And when we poked back at her, it made it seem like we attacked Yvie. Baby, we were safe. I was drinking my cocktails. We were all laughing and everything, and I ain't give a damn. I'm in there laughing, kiking, we were drunk. But Yvie always turned it into something else. And I was like, 'Girl, what's your deal?' And so, she turned it into something else. By the time they started raising multiple questions, that got other girls questioning me and I had them turned up. And this is where I always thought Yvie was playing a game, because the other girls came in and said they all may have to lip-sync and then Yvie started crying and she was like, 'We're back here fighting with each other, and these girls . . . somebody's going to go home.' And I was like, 'Well, bitch, somebody is going to go home, so why are you crying, bitch? You safe this week.'"

Episode 3: "Diva Worship"

For the mini-challenge, contestants are challenged to "seduce" their way backstage at a Seduction concert (Michelle Visage's '90s girl group), with Nina and Ra'Jah snatching the win. For the maxi-challenge, the queens are split into two groups to host a she-vangelical talk show worshipping a diva. Team one is Ariel, Brooke Lynn, Mercedes, Nina, Silky, Vanessa, and Yvie, and their diva is Britney Spears. Team two is A'keria, Honey, Plastique, Ra'Jah, Scarlet, and Shuga, worshipping at the altar of Mariah Carey. Yvie does a brilliant job of playing a nonbeliever who sees the light when Vanjie performs a conversion. On the runway, the category is Fringe, with Yvie wearing their legendary pink jellyfish look. Team Britney Spears is declared the winner, with Nina named the top queen of the week. All six members of Team Mariah are up for elimination; all lip-sync to "Waiting for Tonight" by Jennifer Lopez. Honey Davenport is eliminated.

From Brooke Lynn's perspective, there are two sides to Yvie. There's average, everyday, not on television Yvie, and then there's "Competitor Yvie." "Yvie in real life is chill. They're the nicest, chillest, most easygoing person. And then in a competition setting, I think they kind of go into defense mode a little bit. They get very on edge, I would say. I think they're a good competitor, but in another way, I don't think they're a good competitor because they don't know how to just take criticism from others, you know? So, I think that was really hard. And because they were so different from the rest of the cast, I think they kind of felt alienated, and that everyone else was kind of looking down on them, and making fun of them because they were more of a grunge garbage queen. I don't mean garbage queen in a bad way. I think they kind of felt maybe looked down on or underestimated by the rest of the cast. And I think that put them even more in kind of defense mode, so that when somebody came for them or said something to them, they would just fly off the handle with them."

That dynamic of confrontation showed up as early as episode 2, when Silky asked the other queens who had complained about her to Ru. Yvie questioned why Team "Why It Gotta Be Black, Panther?" was not owning up to the comments. Ariel confessed and Yvie thanked her for being honest but said the rest of the team needed to "step their pussies up" and be truthful. That set Ra'Jah off because she didn't like the hostile energy in the Werk Room, and the two exchanged jabs, particularly about each other's makeup, including Ra'Jah's confessional comment, "an ugly girl can never come for a pretty girl."

Yvie absolutely bears some responsibility for the conflict that occurred between them and Silky, Ra'Jah, and others, but the situation wasn't helped by other contestants who said one thing in private, and one thing in public, if they said anything at all. From Yvie's perspective, "People were like, 'Oh Yvie, I promise you I'm your sister, and I see what you're saying is right. Actually, I agree with you. I just think you maybe brought it up in a wrong way.' Like, we're here to make a reality TV show. I'm not supposed to act annoyed when people are putting on bullshit?" Yvie was bothered by how contestants presented themselves in front of the camera versus how they acted when the cameras weren't rolling.

But that goes both ways, as Silky explains: "I just didn't know when Yvie was being genuine or when they were playing a character." Silky felt that at times Yvie was doing and saying things to get a reaction. "Competitor Yvie" was in charge. And that conflict was hard for Silky, largely because the fight was with another Black queen. "One of the greatest things about being on season 11 is that there was seven Black girls. And one of the things that always hurt me is that me and Yvie always . . . I don't want to say it's beef, because I never had beef with Yvie while we were on the show. We didn't get along, I think that's a better way to say it. But not getting along with a Black queen on the show is one thing that worked my nerves."

Episode 4: "Trump: The Rusical"

For the mini-challenge, the queens impersonate out broadcaster and commentator Rachel Maddow delivering the news from a teleprompter, with Scarlet winning the challenge. For the maxi-challenge, the cast performs one of the infamous Rusicals, specifically *Trump: The Rusical*. Yvie plays Kellyanne Conway and brings to the stage one of the most alarming re-creations of the woman who famously said, with a straight face, that Trump relied on "alternative facts." On the runway, the category is Orange Alert. Yvie wears her stunning Citrus Circus outfit, receiving positive feedback from the judges. Silky wins the challenge. Mercedes and Ra'Jah end up in the bottom and lip-sync to "Living in America" by James Brown. Mercedes is sent home.

The conflict between contestants created tension in the Werk Room. Brooke Lynn says, "It definitely created a little bit more of a tense environment in *Untucked* and in the Werk Room because it felt like it was kind of Yvie against them, and by them, I mean Ra'Jah, Vanjie, A'keria, and Silky especially. And they were very much a clique on the show and very much a little group."

The theme of authenticity is another critically important one in Yvie's experience on *Drag Race*. Yvie prides themself on being real and wants that from everyone else. They want people to be honest. To be themselves. They have no time for people who don't live their authentic lives. And that is plain to see in everything Yvie does and says. But where the issue comes up is when the magic of reality television comes into play and people's willingness to share their entire truth for all the world to see—even if it paints them in a negative light. Who Yvie is, is who the world saw on season 11. Or at least a *part* of who Yvie is. But Yvie doesn't feel that was the case for some of the other cast members, and Yvie saw that as being fake. On Silky, Yvie says, "I was just like, 'You're so fucking put on for this show.' Especially because when we did talk outside of that, even though we come from different walks of life, I respected her viewpoints. Silky wanted to push for better education and the turning red counties blue and shit. Silky is a smart, hardworking individual, but she just wasn't that way on the show. And then she got away with stuff because she has such an amazing personality, and because every guest judge only had to see her once."

But that goes both ways. Yvie *felt* like they were being real, but they were also playing the game. "I wasn't being mean; I was making TV. It's constructed reality. I'm still not any less . . . Well, actually, I do think I'm a little less judgmental. A little. But when we were in a competition setting and people were not being authentic, my character is to be the person who says, 'That's bullshit.' If I'm thinking it in my head, why am I going to hold it there and not say things out loud, which is what the producers wanted anyway. Especially because the one thing I did know about *Drag Race* before this, is that boring girls never make it all the way. And with people like Vanjie and Silky in the room, I wasn't going to be Miss Mary Sunshine. I had to stand out."

Episode 5: "Monster Ball"

For the mini-challenge, the queens turn themselves into a living doll to be besties with RuPaul's doll, and Ra'Jah wins the challenge. For the maxi-challenge, the queens are challenged to bring three looks to the runway as part of the Monster Ball, with categories Trampy Trick or Treater, Witch Please!, and MILF Eleganza. Yvie's first look is the amazing dinosaur costume with claws stuck to their heels. The second look is the black-and-white witch look with their hat covering one eye. And for their third look—the one they made on set—they come out as a sexy voodoo doll. Brooke Lynn wins another design challenge. Ariel and Shuga are in the bottom and lip-sync to "I'm Your Baby Tonight" by Whitney Houston. Ariel sashays away.

Conflicts aside, Yvie takes pride in what they brought to the runway. Their favorite look was episode 3's jellyfish, because it spoke to who Yvie is. "It was the first thing that I had ever done in the local Denver scene that made me feel like I was ready for *Drag Race*. When I wore that out one night, people were gasping and gawking; all night, people were taking pictures, and were like, 'This is one of the coolest things I've ever seen.' From the first time I did that in Denver, I knew I had to wear it on *Drag Race*. And so, when I found a way to fit it into one of the runways, it felt so full circle. Watching Ru gasp—especially because that was week three—it was me coming out hard hitting. I didn't get any judges' feedback the previous week. I crafted that outfit myself in one day and I was so confident in it. It's like what hitting a home run must feel for football players or whatever."

As stressful as it may have been, *Drag Race* fed into Yvie's creative soul. It was an opportunity to create multiple looks and show their artistry to the world. "*Drag Race* felt like the biggest project I'd ever taken on. It was like a senior project in high school, a portfolio project where they say, 'Okay, you have to make ten pieces of art and it can be about whatever you want.' Even though with *Drag Race* they give us a list. But it was that same feeling of 'go in and make the coolest ideas you have and make them come to life however possible.'"

Where the jellyfish was their favorite look, they also have a least favorite. "My least favorites were probably the slime monster [episode 9's Face-Kini Fantasy], because I wanted to wear the heels that I ended up wearing on All Stars 7—the spiked ones—really badly. But I had hurt myself the week before. So, it was not feasible. And that felt disappointing. I liked everything else. I was really proud of everything, and I honestly still liked the slime monster, I was just sad I couldn't wear the shoes with it and give the full presentation I wanted."

Kane Wigham @kanewigham

Episode 6: "The Draglympics"

For the mini-challenge, the contestants do "Galisthenics" with the legendary Love Connie. A'keria and Plastique win the mini-challenge, making them team captains for the maxi-challenge. For the maxi-challenge, the queens perform a freestyle floor performance that includes fanography, voguing, and shablamming. Team A'keria is made up of A'keria, Brooke Lynn, Shuga, Silky, and Yvie. Team Plastique is Plastique, Nina, Ra'Jah, Scarlet, and Vanessa. Yvie performs admirably, considering they turn their ankle mid-performance. On the runway, the category is All That Glitters, and Yvie wears a gorgeous black-and-gold flapper-esque outfit but walks the runway with a cane. A'keria is declared the winner. In the bottom are Ra'Jah and Scarlet, lip-syncing to "Last Dance" by Donna Summer. Scarlet is sent home.

Drag Race was also where Yvie revealed they have hypermobile Ehlers-Danlos syndrome (hEDS). They didn't share that information to get sympathy or for screen time. They shared it because of the circumstances of what was happening in episode 4.

Yanis Marshall—the French dancer and choreographer who rose to stardom on *Britain's Got Talent* by dancing in high heels—was choreographing episode 4's iconic "Trump: The Rusical." Marshall is known for being tough and having the same expectations for every dancer, regardless of body type. If you want to dance a Yanis Marshall piece, you'd best turn it out.

"He had one move that I just knew was going to knock my knees out of place. So, it felt like being the wimpy little nerd in gym class who's like, 'I have a doctor's note.' But also, I love RuPaul. I love this crown. I am not going to intentionally throw myself into something that I know is going to hurt. If there's a chance, then I'm not going to do it. And so that's what that moment was. And then suddenly, his demeanor was like, 'Oh no, that makes sense, darling. I don't want to hurt you. We can't do anything that could hurt somebody with a disease. I understand.' It was a hard challenge. Also, being four weeks in, my body was really starting to feel the stress of being in heels on concrete all day, day after day, after day, after day."

While Yvie revealed they live with hEDS, they didn't feel like it held them back, beyond one runway where they walked with a cane. "I sprained my ankle once, and I couldn't wear my cool heels. But I still got to showcase at least close to the best lip-syncing, and performing, and stunts that I'll ever get to show on such a big, big platform. And I was actually just thinking today about how grateful I am that I got on before I was at where I'm at now, where I have to start cutting things out, where I can feel my body getting weaker. *Drag Race* was literally the beginning of my adult body finally reconciling with the fact that I'm not like everybody else. Because I could vaguely work like everybody else, I could vaguely party like everybody else. And yeah, sure, I'd always go home and take a nap or whatever, but I could keep up. And *Drag Race* was the first place where I was like, 'Oh my God, I actually am physically too weak for this.'"

Episode 7: "From Farm to Runway"

For the mini-challenge, the queens compete in a potato sack race to show off their boob-ography (you can't make this shit up). Yvie competes but in a stationary position, with Nina and Shuga winning. For the maxi-challenge, the contestants create a high-fashion look made from organic materials. Yvie creates a stunning look of reds, oranges, and yellows, described as a sunset in Hawaii. Plastique wins the challenge. A'keria and Ra'Jah are in the bottom and lip-sync to "Strut" by Sheena Easton. Ra'Jah is eliminated.

Week after week, Yvie continued to give it their all, in challenge after challenge that pushed them out of their comfort zone. They may have only won one maxi-challenge, but they were in the top for many of the challenges.

The only low point in the season was, of course, Snatch Game, which for Yvie is still triggering. They struggle with the idea of doing an impersonation and being someone else. Even talking about it causes them stress. Yvie simply doesn't see a world where they can be successful at Snatch Game with the intense pressure to make RuPaul laugh. But even though they stumbled with that challenge, being in the bottom presented an opportunity. It gave them a chance to show RuPaul, the other judges, and most important, the other contestants, what they do best: perform. Yvie went into the lip-sync-for-your-life battle (against Brooke Lynn to Demi Lovato's "Sorry Not Sorry") confident, which can be seen on their face when RuPaul says, "Good luck, and don't fuck it up." Yvie knew what they were going to do.

Win or lose, they were going to leave it all on the stage. The end result was one of the most iconic lip-syncs in the show's history. When the music stopped and RuPaul said, "Shantay, you both stay," Brooke Lynn and Yvie hugged because they had done what they had come to do: show the world they were stars, and peers.

Episode 8: "Snatch Game at Sea"

For the mini-challenge, the contestants pitch their own self-help book and Silky wins. For the maxi-challenge, well, it's Snatch Game at Sea. We all know how that turns out. Yvie's performance sinks. On the runway, the category is Sequins, and Yvie pulls out a Peg Bundy meets Jem and the Holograms pantsuit in greens, reds, and blues. Silky as Ts Madison wins the challenge. Yvie and Brooke Lynn are in the bottom and lip-sync to "Sorry Not Sorry" by Demi Lovato, and after a jaw-dropping performance, we have the season's first double shantay, with neither queen going home.

Yvie did their best in every challenge, and with every runway, and it paid off. On episode 12, they showed off their best drag look—a deep burgundy red velvet floor-length gown with an Yvie twist: a third eye and a third breast. Signature Yvie. And the judges got it, and Yvie was in the top four.

And that was it. The cameras were put away. The lights were turned off. On July 4, 2018, Yvie flew home to sit and wait until the cast was announced on January 24, 2019. For six months and twenty days, they couldn't tell anyone anything. Most people had no idea that Yvie was even on the show. For the few that did know, Yvie couldn't tell them anything lest the spirit of Pepper LaBeija appear out of nowhere and vogue Yvie into an early grave. As Yvie explains, those six months were "really, really hard. I mean, I know that's not a creative word choice, especially since it's something that you can say about basically every step of this process. It was hard knowing my life had changed. And I had the worst panic attack, I think, I've ever had in my life, even worse than Snatch Game, because my friends, and my roommates, and everyone who had helped me get ready were all at my house to welcome me home. And I think my mom and my sisters came by after me literally just disappearing on them and not even telling them where or why I was going to be gone randomly for two months. It was so overwhelming that I went and cried in a closet for a few hours.

"I was feeling so thankful and so relieved to see everyone because I missed them so badly. And I needed a friend, I needed somebody so badly in that experience, and I was so lonely. And then also to get back and now know that I have possibly no genuine friends back home anymore, that even though my family doesn't know it now, their relationship is going to change with me, and people are going to always want something from me now. And I had that panic attack midway between being so thankful to see everyone and looking around and hearing them make little jokes. But jokes that were terrifying to me, like, 'Oh, Yvie's famous now. Yeah, we're all going to get free meat boxes and vacations.'"

What Yvie is referring to is how their relationships would naturally change once *Drag Race* started to air. It's something that occurs with every celebrity. They become part of the public sphere, which changes how people see them. It also changes their friends and family, who get caught in the orbit of the person. That change put Yvie in a position where they started questioning if people were friends with them because they wanted to be friends with them, or because of what they felt Yvie could do for them. And yes, apparently Yvie got a monthly delivery of meat during their reign, and it went to their best friend Teena because Yvie wasn't even home to enjoy it. And that delivery continues to this day, although Yvie is now paying for it.

Episode 9: "L.A.D.P.!"

For the mini-challenge, the queens read each other to filth in the much-loved Reading Challenge, with Brooke Lynn taking home the win. For the maxi-challenge, the queens turn out an improv challenge in the comedy police sketch Los Angeles Drag Patrol. Yvie and A'keria bring to life the twerking girls corner disturbance as mother and daughter. On the runway, the category is Face-Kini Fantasy, and Yvie brings us her creature from the black lagoon runway diva look. A'keria wins the challenge, and Plastique and Vanessa are in the bottom, lip-syncing to "Hood Boy" by Fantasia. Plastique is sent packing.

Post–*Drag Race* reality set in. Yvie had to get back to living some semblance of a life, until the cast announcement, and all the fun/chaos began. "I transitioned back into real life. But it was all surreal because I couldn't pay my bills. My roommate Morgan was the breadwinner for the whole house, for the most part. For a month I was depressed, and so shaken, and also scared, because now I'm thinking about the post–*Drag Race* stuff that I had never thought about. Suddenly I'm getting emails from managers who are like, 'Hey, I'd really love to meet with you. When can we fly you out? I'll take you on a little mini tour right now and have you do a couple of shows just so you can see what it would be like to work with me. I'll have you work with a photographer.'" It's worth noting here that at this point, no one should have known that Yvie was even on *Drag Race*, let alone in the top four. But there are some loose lips in the *Drag Race* world, and people find things out. Reddit is a treasure trove of *Drag Race* tea.

"So, there's mourning the past, and also this fear and inability to move forward. Inability, because I didn't ever want to work another job that wasn't drag again if I'm about to be a fucking drag superstar. After a month of being depressed and not being able to feed myself, I went back to the club and picked up a day position. And they were like, 'You look like you don't even care about this job.' And I'm like, 'Yeah, because I'm on fucking *Drag Race*.'

"And it's extra bizarre because when I say the world knows, the world knows. I slowly start getting back into doing as much drag as I can in the Denver scene to keep myself sane. And everybody and their fucking mother knows. Of course they know. No drag queen disappears in the months when RuPaul films unless they're going to film *Drag Race*. And I have these people coming up to me and being like, 'Hey girl, I just want to say I'm really proud of you and don't forget me.' You feel how fake the world gets when you're on TV."

Yvie's suspicions were confirmed. People who had doubted Yvie's talent and disregarded them as a drag artist suddenly were there to support them. Or worse, people who had never paid any attention to Yvie were trying to curry favor with them. All this before the show even aired. "That was the hardest thing to get over in those six months, because once *Drag Race* did finally start airing, it was like I didn't even have to worry about the past anymore. I'd gotten into a few arguments with my closest friends and a few arguments with my family, breaking down to them about how I didn't have time to care about them as much as they care about me. And how the dynamic between a famous person and a not famous person is very annoying because it does exist. And it is set in stone, where unfortunately, as long as my name is in the news, is on TV, is doing things, you're probably going to be thinking about me more than I am thinking of you. Which is a hard dynamic to grasp, and which is why it surprises me that Doug loves me at all."

They're not wrong, especially for a new celebrity. Yvie was trying to figure out a brand-new world, and friends and family can be there for the journey, but they don't experience it the same way. There's the challenge of being on social media, of being recognized in the grocery store, of having relationships and knowing the difference between a genuine friend and a friend who's there to get something from them. The family and friends you have before stardom are the people you can rely on to be there when you sort it all out.

When *Drag Race* started to air, Yvie made good on their promise and started hosting viewing parties at Tracks. And as they explain, they were a bit painful, but at the same time, it helped with their healing because it gave them the opportunity to prove themselves, whether they needed to or not. "That year, specifically while my season was airing, is probably the hardest I have ever worked my body. Everywhere I was going, I was pulling every trick I could, doing the absolute most I could to try and show people, 'Hey, I'm going to be worth something. Even though I'm not killing it in the show.'" Hello, imposter syndrome.

Episode 10: "Dragracadabra"

For the mini-challenge, the queens play a game called Balls to the Wall where they pair up with Pit Crew members to transfer balls to a basket using different parts of their bodies. Vanessa wins the mini-challenge. For the maxi-challenge, the girls team up to perform a magic show for a live studio audience. The teams are Da Black Magic, made up of A'keria, Silky, Vanessa, and Yvie; and The Mighty Tucks, made up of Brooke Lynn, Nina, and Shuga. On the runway, the category is Caftan Realness, with Yvie serving an epic yellow drapey goddess look. Nina wins the maxi-challenge. Shuga and Vanessa are in the bottom, lip-syncing to "No More Drama" by Mary J. Blige. Shuga is sent home.

The season continued to air, and in early May 2019, Yvie returned to Los Angeles to film the finale. That episode is shot two to three weeks before it airs, in front of a jam-packed theater, ensuring that the top four contestants aren't revealed too far in advance. "By the time we got to film the finale, I was already exhausted. All the rest of the top four were exhausted because we had all had a whole season of the online comments, and the bullshit, and the comparisons. The wildest part about this finale was it was going to be this catharsis for it all. But it still wasn't going to be over. Just that step of it. And when I got told that we were getting ready to film the finale, I just prepared for what I thought would be the best way to close off my senior high school portfolio that I had presented so far. I had to make masterpieces. You can't step backward, and you can't be underwhelming after a season of jaw-dropping."

Filming the finale goes from the sublime to the ridiculous. The first part—a lip-sync for the crown between two pairs of contestants—is the sublime. It's sublime because it's where all four of the queens got to thrive: performing in front of a crowd. Silky selected Brooke Lynn to compete against, and they took on "Bootylicious" by Destiny's Child, and Brooke Lynn prevailed. Then it was Yvie against A'keria to "SOS" by Rihanna. Yvie's first look was what can only be described as a patchwork of puppets as done by Alexander McQueen. A'keria put on a fierce performance, but ultimately Yvie was victorious. Then it came down to Yvie and Brooke Lynn, performing "The Edge of Glory" by Lady Gaga. Yvie wore an eye-conic [See what I did there? Because they wore a third eye?] brown-and-gold, floor-length gown with a huge, mirrored headpiece. The two of them battled it out in a lip-sync for the crown. And the winner was . . . both of them. Sort of.

It's well known that they film multiple versions of the finale and of the queens giving their acceptance speech. They do this to keep the winner a secret right up until the last minute. "It was all acting in that moment, which is why I fucked up my lines both times because I didn't feel like the winner at that moment. There were plenty of points in that night when I did. But when you know that you have to put on a show of winning and you have to say your little crowning words, it's the most inauthentic that reality TV had gotten up to that point. It felt like nothing. Especially after the lip-sync that Brooke and I did, it was very reminiscent of finishing 'Sorry Not Sorry,' where we were on this even playing field. We looked over at each other and were like, 'Oh my God. Girl, we did that. This is all done now.' All of that chaotic bullshit is done and it's literally all out of our hands. Now we finally get to experience what Soju got to experience when they said, 'Well, my *Drag Race* journey is over.'" And it was over. At least for a few weeks.

Episode 11: "Bring Back My Queens!"

For the mini-challenge, the queens attempt to make Ru slap them by insulting her in the game Slap Out of It. Brooke Lynn manages to offend the most, taking home the win. For the maxi-challenge, the eliminated queens return for a makeover challenge. Yvie is paired with Scarlet. On the runway, the category is Drag Family Values. Yvie and Scarlet wear matching denim-strip outfits but Yvie receives poor critiques from the judges. The queens are asked who should be sent home, and five queens pick Yvie (Soju,

Silky, A'keria, Vanessa, and Nina) while the rest name Silky. Brooke Lynn wins the challenge and Yvie is safe. Nina and Silky are in the bottom and lip-sync to "No Scrubs" by TLC. Nina is told to sashay away.

Nearly immediately, doubt crept in. Yvie went back to their hotel thinking Brooke Lynn had won. Teena was with Yvie after the filming of the finale. As Teena explains, "I get back to the hotel room with Yvie and the mood was somber. The mood was, 'Well, is RuPaul going to let a Black person win? Will a Black queen be able to be crowned? RuPaul's not going to let that happen.' We have a room full of drag queens and they're just all wringing their hands, and Yvie's very nervous and quiet. And I said to Yvie, 'I just watched you take the crown; I know I did. Why are we not partying it up?' They're like, 'I don't know, I don't know, maybe I didn't win.'"

As Yvie explains, "I didn't think I'd won, despite the amazing audience reaction I had, and despite the fact that I was beating Brooke Lynn in the polls online. I didn't think I'd won because on paper Brooke Lynn did better; she won more challenges; she had perfect runways that never missed the mark. But more importantly, we were in the swell of the fan-base era, where the fans are going to choose who wins. And even though I was moving people emotionally or whatever, Brooke Lynn did the drag that more people could relate to."

It's interesting to see different perspectives from people who experience the same thing. As far as Brooke Lynn was concerned,

"I'd been very on top, and all of a sudden, well, I was the worst one and Yvie was the best one. Yvie was just everything, they were so unique, they were so different, they were so talented. And all of those things are very true, and they also killed the verse in the music video [RuPaul's 'Queens Everywhere']. Their verse was incredible, and their performance was incredible. And they were just so different and unique from everyone else on our cast that it truly was like an underdog story. They had a slow burn to the top, whereas I started out on top, and I had a couple of missteps along the way. But my story just wasn't as interesting as Yvie's, and quite frankly, my drag wasn't as interesting as theirs. I'm a gorgeous drag queen, but besides the dance thing, I'm not super, super unique, where Yvie is completely unique and completely their own. So, all of those things, in addition to the way the judges were praising them, just kind of made me realize that when you're watching TV and you're watching that final episode and then you watch the finale, it just kind of makes sense, you know?"

Jump forward a few weeks to May 30, 2019. The top four gathered at the Levi's flagship store in San Francisco for the airing of the finale. By that time, the cast was already back together rehearsing for the season 11 tour and had performed their first show four days prior. Yvie's crowning was less about an exciting turn of events and more about exhaustion. "By the time we got to San Francisco I was just ready for it to be over. I was exhausted. We did the finale, and then two weeks later we did DragCon LA, and immediately left on tour. So, it was the first time I was working like I've been working ever since, a full-on ass Ru girl. Also,

Breakfast Jones @breakfastjones

I think for the first time I was really, really concerned about winning, because there was a fifty-fifty chance that day. Because I was so close, and the win was right there. And because both endings were filmed, it could be either one of us. I don't know, I was just sweating, watching the whole thing. Very, very nervous to see how whatever I was feeling in that moment translated because when we did 'Sorry Not Sorry' there was this energy in the room, like, 'Wow, that was one of the most remarkable things we've ever seen. And of course, you're both going to stay,' even though we were just in the studio and not in front of an audience. It was easy for me to know what Ru's response was going to be.

"But to watch the final lip-sync, we knew they could edit it whatever way they wanted to, to make it look the best for whoever they wanted. And I was so unaware of Brooke, other than the fact that she had on a mirrored cat suit and did her dance moves. I was thinking, 'I don't know how it's all going to look at the end, and if this one performance is still going to be enough to propel me.'"

Again, Brooke Lynn's perspective differs from Yvie's. "My goal going into the finale was to get to the final lip-sync. And I knew Yvie was going to have some weird, different thing. I didn't really expect them to come out in a gown and literally just stand there while I was jumping around them. So that was, again, very smart of Yvie because it just made them look like the queen. Where I was just kind of the jumping bean. And I was performing, but I wasn't . . . I don't know, it's kind of what people expected me to do as well."

In the end, what Yvie did was more than enough. Whether it was because the fans voted for Yvie more than they did for Brooke Lynn, or that RuPaul or the producers of the show felt Yvie's lip-sync was better, or . . . who knows? Whatever the reasoning, Yvie took home the crown.

In retrospect, as Yvie looks back on the season, they're satisfied with what they see. They see it as truthful. There is a history of contestants on *Drag Race* blaming producers for giving them a poor edit that didn't reflect what really happened. So much so that in 2022, RuPaul released the song "Blame It on the Edit," including the lyric, "Go on and take the credit, bitch, you the one who said it, bitch." Yvie doesn't feel that way. As they explain, "I was fine with the editing because it was honest. It told the story of what was happening in those moments. Including the moments where I didn't look like a good guy, which was really important to me because I know that I wasn't one hundred percent in the right. I felt like I was being gaslit by all of the girls, like, 'Oh no, you're just acting out, you're just doing too much.' And then to watch the show back and see everyone being pissed and annoyed at Silky from day one really set the tone for me watching the rest of the season. And then getting to see just some of the things that they said behind my back. They were really mean-spirited. And I'm not some fragile little butterfly or whatever. I've gotten called everything they said and worse. But it was just shocking to me, because the lowest blow I threw all season long was calling Silky untalented. That was the closest I came to actually personally insulting someone rather than just stating a fact. Silky is incredibly talented."

You may think that Yvie would have regrets about their time on *Drag Race*, but not really. "All the things I regret about that season were things that were out of my control, because I think they ultimately influenced my entire experience there. I regret not making close sisters and making friends with the girls." But as Lashauwn Beyond from season 4 said, "This is not RuPaul's best friends' race."

YVIE'S TOP 5 WAYS TO SNAG YOUR DREAM DATE

1. Ask them lots of questions. Confuse them.
2. Meet on an app, hook up at their place, and just don't leave.
3. Go to church.
4. Be yourself.
5. Lie.

Yvie, post
winning *RPDR*

Yvie, post winning *RPDR*

From *RPDR All Stars,
All Winners*, "The Pleather
Principle Look"

From *RPDR All Stars,*
All Winners, "Knitty Knitty
Bang Bang Look"

From *RPDR All Stars,*
All Winners, "Veiled It Look"

From *RPDR All Stars, All Winners,* "Drag Race Gives Back Variety Extravaganza"

Yvie with
husband, Doug

The OG Avon Eve

Avon Eve performing
at a queer masquerade in
a basement of Auraria
Campus of Metropolitan
State University of Denver

An early look for Avon Eve

An early look for Avon Eve

A young Avon LaRue practicing her mug

Avon Eve as Storm from *X-Men*

Avon Eve performing at Rainbow Alley's "Queer Prom,"
Metropolitan State University of Denver, 2013

Yvie walking the runway in Studio Yoshida with
designer Kotomi Yoshida, Red Ball, 2015

Yvie as her cat, Lucky

From *RPDR*, season 11, "Caftan Realness Look"

Behind the scenes with Yvie's reunion look for *RPDR*, season 11

From *RPDR,* season 11, "Best Drag Look"

Yvie with their father, Sheps

Backstage at *RuPaul's Drag Race Live!*, 2021

Interview on set of *RuPaul's Drag Race Live!*, 2021

Behind the scenes at the promo shoot for *RPDR All Stars, All Winners*

Yvie performing at a queer party at 2 a.m. in Miami in her *RPDR* Grand Finale Look

Yvie "working out" the stage of the winners after-party, Rupaul's DragCon UK, 2023

Captured by Marco Ovando backstage during Werq The World, 2019

Little Jovan turning his first look as the Jolly Green Giant

Jovan working on his floor routine

Jovan jamming on the piano

A teenage Jovan with mom, Jessyca, and sisters, Lya and Cheyenne

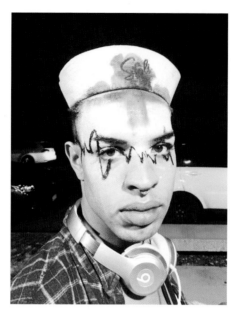

Jovan as a manager at Tracks Nightclub, 2017

Jovan as a manager with some patrons of Tracks

Jovan promoting Tracks

Yvie with bestie Teena backstage at The Odd Hour (Yvie's first foray into club promotion), Tracks, 2016

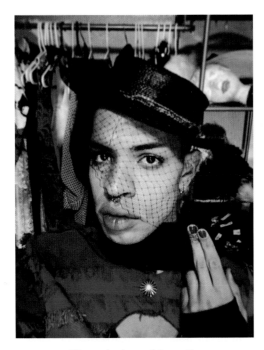

The early days of Avon Eve

Jovan with DSA friends

Jovan and mom, Jessyca

CHAPTER 6

OVERNIGHT SENSATION: LIFE AFTER *DRAG RACE*

As contestants move through the competition, there are emotional stages they go through. For Yvie, it went like this: There was the episode 1 terror of "please don't let me be the first to go home." Then the ecstasy of winning the second maxi-challenge. Then with each passing episode that they were safe or in the top, and they watched their competition sashaying away, confidence started to build as their momentum did. Then there was the crash of reality with Snatch Game, where it was nearly all over. Then relief, followed by more confidence stemming from more momentum. Then they got to the finale and realized they had a shot at winning. Then they won! It was an emotional roller coaster that for Yvie mostly went up. But like everything in life, what goes up, must come down. Even before the finale was filmed, Yvie and the rest of the cast went into rehearsals for the season 11 tour.

Yvie and all of the season 11 cast returned to Los Angeles to start rehearsals. It was the first time they'd seen each other in more than six months. It was an opportunity to reconnect, and really get to know one another without the cameras rolling.

Asia O'Hara, the drag legend and Ru girl who finished in the top four of *Drag Race* season 10, was playing the role of host for the tour. Her first impressions of Yvie didn't quite align with the Yvie that the world was getting to know on *Drag Race*. "I remember that first day, I came in toward the end of the rehearsal. And I remember Yvie was having some issues with their joints and they were in some pain, so they were a little subdued. Everybody else was being loud and rambunctious. And Yvie was very polite, but they were very quiet and somewhat to themself. They didn't seem frazzled, or bothered, or in their feelings, or anything. They weren't, in my opinion, in the same headspace that a lot of us that are in the top four are during that point in our season."

Asia's observations are an astute reflection of where Yvie was mentally once *Drag Race* started to air. What the world was seeing on their television screens—the yelling, the conflict, the drama, the heat—was not reflected in the reality of who Yvie was or is. "Competitor Yvie" was gone, and now the cast was getting "Real-Life Yvie," but this new Yvie was processing a lot of new feelings and generally feeling overwhelmed.

The season 11 cast tour started on May 26, 2019, as part of DragCon in Los Angeles, and on June 1, 2019, Yvie woke up with the title of America's Next Drag Superstar. Their entire world had changed overnight, leaving Yvie feeling empty.

May 26, 2019
First performance of season 11 cast tour

May 30, 2019
Yvie is crowned winner of season 11 of *RuPaul's Drag Race*

"I poured so much energy into *Drag Race*. Before I ever got on, I was working for the kind of validation that the *idea* of winning *Drag Race* would bring. I think a part of the human condition is always having these intangible goals, always having this ideal life that's just a little bit better than what you're living right now. But there's so much that comes with the dynamic of even getting on *Drag Race* that changes your perspective about dreams versus reality. It shows you that when your dreams come true, there's still life to live. And at least for me, there was this dramatic shift in how I felt I was perceived by the world, and how I felt I could exist in it. So, when I was crowned, I was genuinely thrilled. I obviously wanted this. But there was this emptiness."

Yvie, truth be told, hadn't considered what life would be like after being on the show, let alone winning. The way they process information and experiences hadn't allowed for it. Now they were faced with some challenging questions. They achieved their goal, but they were on tour, trying to keep up with a grueling schedule, surrounded by their castmates whom they had beaten out for the crown, desperate for a moment to pause and take it all in. "I just realized that the way I worked and how I was processing all the changes in my life up to that point wasn't stable. There wasn't any real stability because everything was built off of these dreams and ideals. And on top of all the pressures of feeling like I needed to live up to something now, it was strange to hit the top and start realizing that there's still more to go.

"There were points in the competition when I thought I was going to win. There were points in filming the finale where I was like, 'Oh, yeah. I'm going to win.' It's such an intangible dream that at least for me, it was hard to plan for what was next. Because everything I had planned for the future just didn't work out like I thought. I thought my friend, roommate, assistant was going to be my manager, and help me on the road, and take care of my affairs, and that was chaotic. I just thought everything was going to be different. And it was, but in a way that was a lot harder to handle in an overnight fashion than I ever could have imagined."

Yvie thought everything was going to be different as it relates to their roommates Teena and Morgan—and specifically Morgan. As Yvie describes it, the character of "Yvie Oddly" was as much part of Morgan as it was part of Yvie. "I literally could not in any way have gone through that whole experience without Morgan, because he was the person who first started believing in me when I competed locally in Denver. He started putting together ideas, and helped craft my numbers and outfits, and would try and get me shows. So when I got on *Drag Race* it was not only a win for me, but it was a win for us."

As much as Yvie is extremely independent, they're also fiercely loyal to family, and Teena and Morgan were part of their chosen family. Winning *Drag Race* was a collective success. And they felt that success would not only benefit them but would benefit Morgan as well. But the pressure of fame and success for Morgan, even peripherally, had a different outcome.

"I felt like I lost control of my life," Yvie says. "And that's what really became the issue, down to my personal relationships. That's why I posted to the fans and to the world, 'I don't want to fucking take photos after I just broke my pussy on the floor for you for hours.' That's where all of that came from. My days, for the first time, were not at all in my control. The routine was get up and go to the gig, catch the flight, do the number that's going to please the most people, do the laugh that everybody loves, listen to the same sentences over and over again: 'I was rooting for you from the start.' 'I didn't like you at first, but then I came around when you did this or that.'

"I felt incapable of handling it all. There was a long period where both Teena and Morgan were taking care of the business end of my business for me. They were handling all the merch sales, they were talking to my managers, answering emails, making sure itineraries were in place."

Control becomes another theme in Yvie's trajectory of success, and specifically, the loss of it. "Yvie Oddly" became a commodity, and Yvie the person felt like they were losing control over their choices. And there is a price that can come with that, as Yvie saw with their social media. "I gave most of it up to Morgan. He was the best person to run my social media, because that's what he had done at Tracks. And where I started having issues is, I realized it's one thing to give up control of your schedule or give up control of how you dress or whatever. But to give up control of your voice is, at least for me, very dangerous, because then things can become inauthentic. It is lying. For me, it's the biggest lie you can have, because the most truth I have comes from my thoughts and my words. Morgan made a few big mistakes specifically on my Twitter. He accidentally started a beef between me and the girls from *The Boulet Brothers' Dragula*, who I love, by making a joke and calling them trash or something. He posted some whiny rant to Raja and Raven about them booting my jellyfish look on *Fashion Photo RuView*, because he thought it was iconic. But this is where I started thinking, 'Okay, I understand, because I'm passionate about these things too. But if I'm going to be getting in hot water on social media, which is how you have to move through the world, I would prefer it to be coming from my mouth.'

"The biggest challenge was that Morgan had things that he wanted, which is understandable. He had dreams that he wanted and things that he needed to get out of this experience, which I was bitter about because it felt like he was using me. And one of those things was his sex life. He followed and talked to so many random guys on my account. And then he gave me two drag children that I'd never accepted by just halfway jokingly saying online, 'Yes, I'm your mother now.' What he didn't realize was how much of an impact it would have on those people, and how much I had to be responsible for them afterward. He was jealous that I was getting so much attention, rightfully so. Ultimately, it just wasn't a good way to mix my personal life and my work life. Especially because he was my roommate and traveling with me."

Yvie found themself in a predicament. They felt their win was a collective success and wanted to include their besties in that win. Add to that, they didn't feel like they could do it alone because at that level

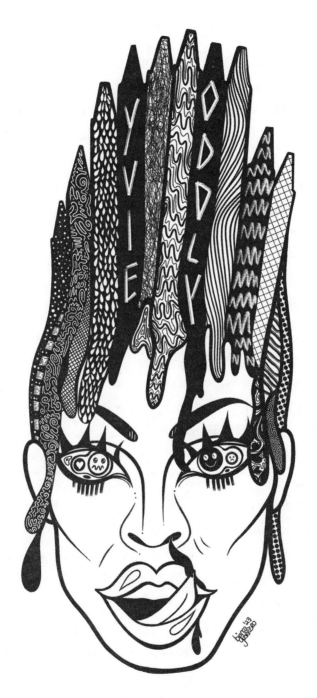

Bianca Guerrero biancaguerrero.com

of celebrity and success, there are simply too many demands for your time. Success came so fast that they didn't have the systems in place to manage it. They needed to rely on other people to help with the sheer volume of work, yet struggled with the idea of giving up control.

"I saw the repercussions of all of this. I just felt like I couldn't do it alone. But that also robbed me of having anything under my control. Teena and Morgan bought my clothes, they made my outfits, they decided what was happening. Because any time we got a new email and it'd be like, 'You have a booking for this amazing opportunity that should bring you so much joy,' I'd just be like, 'I don't know what to do.' I won *Drag Race*. I put everything into that. All of our energy went into these stupid fucking outfits, and these ideas for these performances. I don't have anything else to give. Especially seeing how flimsy the love that you get can be, and always is.

"It was honestly too much. First of all, it was too much of an expectation for us all to be roommates. To live together and have to have this communal tribal mindset of 'if Yvie is succeeding, then we are all succeeding' was too much. And then add to that the responsibilities and pressures on people who were never meant to handle all of them, because they were just learning about this world like I was. We didn't have our Ru girlfriends that taught us how this shit goes. We were scraping by, and in ways, they both—Teena and Morgan—still got what they wanted. I'd say Teena more so, because somehow they adjusted their expectations to reality pretty quickly when all the shit hit the fan: They got more followers on Instagram, they started a house of their own. I also think it was harder on Morgan because I placed more weight on him, having him do more things to manage me, to help direct my voice and my ideas to people."

May 26, 2019
First performance of season 11 cast tour

May 30, 2019
Yvie is crowned winner of season 11
of *RuPaul's Drag Race*

June 2019
Filming of *Yvie's Odd School* in Los Angeles

July 10, 2019
Yvie goes back out on tour

In addition to navigating the changes in their personal relationships, Yvie was also trying to figure out their future. In the middle of the season 11 cast tour, they landed in LA to film *Yvie's Odd School*—a World of Wonder production. They weren't contractually obligated to make the show, but it felt like an opportunity they had to pursue to prove they deserved to win *Drag Race*. "I was involved in the creative process, but they were talking to a zombie. They were throwing ideas at me like, 'Oh, you should go visit all these weird places in LA and do all these weird things. Or you can just have this crafty show that teaches people how to do your drag and be authentic to yourself or whatever.' And I actually was passionate about that idea, but there was just no space to tap into my creativity. Because when I went to film that, it was right after my first month of touring, after winning, after being exhausted, after dealing with all of these social changes in my life. And I get there with whatever the fuck I'd had in my suitcase and they're like, 'All right, so we just got you some materials and you're going to be creative. And this is going to be fun,' and threw me into it. And some people may be able to make gold like that, but I was so fucking unpassionate about that whole project from the second we started filming. And it's strange, because you can tell that the idea behind that is something I would like to do. But I made that because I felt like I had to.

"There are very few decisions in my career that I regret. For me, I'm glad I did *Odd School* because I learned that I don't want to do that. If I want to have a project like that, I want it to be on my terms, I want to be in charge. Don't throw me whatever random guest stars that you're trying to sell. I want to be in charge of my own vision. That's why I became a drag queen: I'm selfish."

May 26, 2019
First performance of season 11 cast tour

May 30, 2019
Yvie is crowned winner of season 11
of *RuPaul's Drag Race*

June 2019
Filming of *Yvie's Odd School* in Los Angeles

July 10, 2019
Yvie goes back out on tour

September 6, 2019
Last performance of season 11 cast tour
in New York City

September 7–9, 2019
DragCon New York

September 11, 2019
Werq the World kickoff, Kansas City

Following the filming of *Odd School*, Yvie went back out on the road to complete the season 11 cast tour. That wrapped up on September 6 in New York City, leading directly into DragCon NYC. Two days later, Yvie set out on the Werq the World tour, produced by World of Wonder and Voss Events—the production and management company that represents Yvie. It kicked off on September 11, 2019, in Kansas City and involved forty-five performances in sixty-two days in Canada and the United States, with one additional stop in Mexico City on November 26 of that same year. That is a tough schedule for the most seasoned of road warriors: waking up every day in a different city in a strange bed, performing and leaving it all on the stage, then getting on a bus, train, or airplane to travel to the next city, before doing it all over again. But for someone who was new to the road, it was grueling.

"It was ridiculous in every way possible, because this felt like the peak of what I had been working toward beyond *Drag Race*. You're performing for thousands of people every night, and you have to give the most drama to fill that space. I got to do what I wanted by just painting myself green and getting back at least a little bit of what Yvie meant to me. So there was the high of that. But also, it was the first time that I was so deadly lonely. Touring has become easier for me now, but that first tour I was lonely because all of the girls, minus Vanjie and Plastique, had done tours before, and they were like, 'This is how this works,' and 'Oh my God, remember that story?' It's not like anyone was trying to be exclusive, but once again, I felt like I had no place to fit in, and no soul to do anything with.

"And it was also the longest period I had gone without seeing Doug. This was our first time not seeing each other for multiple months since we had started dating. So, I was experiencing so many different kinds of loneliness and otheredness in one. And on top of it, because I was still in my reigning year and for some strange reason still trying to prove why I got crowned, I was doing the absolute fucking most with my body, and this was when I had already known and started experiencing things actually breaking down. And I still decided to do a whole five-minute dance number with a two-minute contortion break in the middle. And I felt the repercussions of that. Just trying to put out all of my energy and give out everything for everyone while also feeling so by myself, so alone."

For Yvie, the Werq the World tour can be described as the "still trying to prove why I got crowned" tour. This is where the imposter syndrome was running rampant. Even after being crowned, and performing for tens of thousands of screaming fans, they still felt like they had to prove their worth. That belief is a battle that continues to this day, although it has gotten better. "Honestly, what I've had to unlearn every day since then is that I already did it. I got the crown. Whether or not it was right, whether or not it was good, whether or not it was the way it was supposed to be done, it doesn't matter because I already did it. So now, I remind myself, just do the things that make you happy about drag, like you did when you started doing drag. Now I am not working to please the people half as hard as I'm working to please *me*, and it seems to be pleasing the people."

May 26, 2019

First performance of season 11 cast tour

May 30, 2019

Yvie is crowned winner of season 11
of *RuPaul's Drag Race*

June 2019

Filming of *Yvie's Odd School* in Los Angeles

July 10, 2019

Yvie goes back out on tour

✈ 🚋🚂 🚗 ✈ 🚋🚂 🚗 ✈

September 6, 2019

Last performance of season 11 cast tour
in New York City

September 7–9, 2019

DragCon New York

September 11, 2019

Werq the World kickoff, Kansas City

✈ 🚋🚂 🚗 ✈ 🚋🚂 🚗 ✈

November 26, 2019

Werq the World wraps, Mexico City

Vegas changed everything. Following the season 11 cast tour, and the Werq the World tour, Yvie was cast in the newly created *RuPaul's Drag Race Live* in Las Vegas. *Drag Race Live* can be best described as a "day job" of drag. Five shows a week, always at the same venue, and in a professional stage production. "When I say that Vegas changed everything, it was the first time I made the decision to take back control. Morgan was like, 'Should I come out there with you?' And I was like, 'No, no. I'm going to live here. You guys handle my stuff at home. I'll still pay the rent for you guys or whatever, and I'll live this Vegas life.' And then the pandemic hit, and I had to move back home, with Doug now also living with me. Me and Doug moved back into that three-bedroom, one-bathroom apartment with Teena and their partner, and Morgan and this guy he was seeing at the time. So, it was so many people and so much tension in one house because we were all fucking trapped there. As soon as I could, I moved into a different unit in that apartment complex.

And that really fractured everything with everyone because that was when we all—me, Morgan, and Teena—essentially had a roommate breakup talk. For three hours, shouting in our court-yard about all of what had been going wrong with our dreams and expectations from this experience versus the reality. There was a long period of time where Morgan was bitter that I essen-tially took our baby—even though it's mine—and got all the success and fun from it. And then he went back to serving jobs and shit. But there's still a note of that bitterness in our relation-ship. I mean, he's so important to me that I'd never want him to not be a part of my life. And things have gotten way better with us living on our own and being able to grow through our trauma and issues. And so, removing all of that from our friendship has given me the space to love and appreciate him again."

May 26, 2019

First performance of season 11 cast tour

May 30, 2019

Yvie is crowned winner of season 11

of *RuPaul's Drag Race*

June 2019

Filming of *Yvie's Odd School* in Los Angeles

July 10, 2019

Yvie goes back out on tour

✈ 🚃🚅 🚗 ✈ 🚃🚅 🚗 ✈

September 6, 2019

Last performance of season 11 cast tour

in New York City

September 7–9, 2019

DragCon New York

September 11, 2019

Werq the World kickoff, Kansas City

✈ 🚃🚅 🚗 ✈ 🚃🚅 🚗 ✈

November 26, 2019

Werq the World wraps, Mexico City

December 1, 2019

Rehearsals begin for *Drag Race Live*

Yvie found themselves trying to figure out who Yvie was going to be post–*Drag Race*. Prior to being cast on the show, they were desperate for the attention. They wanted people to see them and celebrate their artistry. But when reality set in, and they couldn't

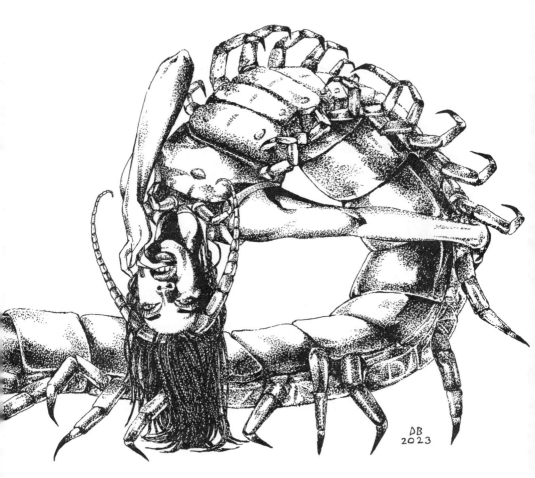

Diana B 📷 *@dottybonbon*

walk down the street without being recognized, it started to be less appealing.

Yvie isn't unrealistic and acknowledges that they need their fans. Without their fans, they wouldn't be where they are today. But that fame comes at a cost—a level of pressure that feels like they're carrying the world on their shoulders. The pressure to show the world that they deserved to be crowned America's Next Drag Superstar. The pressure to satisfy their fans. The pressure to be doing the best drag of their life. However, there's only so long that a person can stand that level of pressure before they crack under the weight of it.

YVIE'S BIGGEST PET PEEVES

1. Being forced to interact with people's dogs. It literally puts the pet in my pet peeve.

2. Bad sidewalk walkers. If you're gonna take up the whole-ass sidewalk then at least work it, bitch! Like sissy that sidewalk; I've got places to be!

3. Sweet & savory flavors. Why are humans so obsessed with them?! Orange chicken, BBQ flavor, and every single fast-food chain's "special sauce" can burn in hell with the people who invented them.

4. Brightly lit bars and clubs. I should never be able to see everyone and everything everywhere at night! That's what daytime is for.

5. Jinkx's dick jokes. I promise you I don't want to hear them ever again in any context.

CHAPTER 7

HONEYMOON IN VEGAS: RUPAUL'S DRAG RACE LIVE!

The life of a drag queen, particularly a successful Ru girl who tours, may seem exciting, but the truth of the matter is, it ain't all that. You live out of a suitcase. You're in a different city every night, which means a different hotel, a different bed, and often a different time zone, let alone a different continent. You're far away from your friends and family, and heaven help you if there's another cast member you don't get along with.

The idea of a stable opportunity to do what you love is very enticing, as it was for Yvie when the idea of *Drag Race Live* came up. While on tour with Werq the World, Yvie and a number of other queens were approached by Brandon Voss, founder and CEO of Voss Events (producers of Werq the World), about the concept of doing a Las Vegas residency. Yvie jumped at the chance because, in their eyes, it was an opportunity to do something that hadn't been done before. While there have always been drag shows in Vegas, there had never been a major show on the Strip that was headlined by drag queens. More important, it was an opportunity for Yvie to stay in one place and get the stability they so desperately needed. No hotels. No suitcases. Just a consistent experience, doing drag in one place.

After the chaos of 2019, the opportunity to do a show like *Drag Race Live* was a blessing for Yvie. It provided a level of stability that they were missing, along with the opportunity to be part of something new and exciting. Yvie's feeling was shared by the other cast members. As Asia O'Hara explains, the first word that came to mind when they saw the cast list was "Love. Prior to *Drag Race Live*, Yvie and I had toured on Werq the World together and that was really where I felt like I got to know them as a person."

Cast member Naomi Smalls felt similarly: "When the cast of *Drag Race Live* was first announced, I was so ecstatic just because it was pretty much all my friends. And then there was Derrick Barry, who . . . we weren't necessarily friends when we got cast for *Drag Race Live*, but we had familiarity with each other."

The experience of putting up a Vegas revue was a new one for Yvie and the entire cast, made up of Yvie, Asia, Naomi, Derrick Barry, Kameron Michaels, and Vanessa Vanjie Mateo. "I had never been a part of a production like this," Yvie says. "I had done theater before, so I was used to how theater productions work. I went out to LA, where we worked on some choreography for a week. And then a month later, we all moved to Vegas. We maybe had a month or so, but we had to build the entire show. The writers were still writing. We were trying to find places where the script or a song fit or didn't fit. And how does this work? What's the punch line there? It was literally the first six of us building a theater production with the crew and creative team, who also seemed like it was their first time building out a theater production. A drag show and a play or musical are two very different experiences and require different things. When the writers had written the original script, they had expected us to have a million costume changes. And there still are many during the show, but it's much more reasonable now. Quick changes in theater are easier than quick changes in drag." None of that is terribly surprising. *Drag Race Live* represented something completely new. They were taking *RuPaul's Drag Race*, turning it into a scripted show, and putting it on a stage in Las Vegas. There isn't an instruction manual for the "reality TV contest to scripted musical" process, or it would have been done already.

Asia's perspective on the experience is similar. "You never really know what to expect when you do new projects. So, when we got to Vegas, it was a lot more stressful because Ru was there, the executive producers from World of Wonder and Voss Events were there, Jamal Sims was there, Leland, who wrote all the music, was there. Everybody wanted their contributions to be perfect. It was a lot of pressure for all six of us because we were all trying to do right by this work of art. Everybody was stressed, and everybody was kind of dealing with their stress in different ways. So, it was not as smooth as it was when we first started rehearsing."

For Yvie, the opportunity presented so much more than just a consistent paycheck. It was an opportunity to catch their breath and get to know themself as an artist again. "In my home life, there was the autonomy of having my own space and feeling in control of my life. Vegas was the first time in my life I had ever lived all on my own. And I had the space and the time to do my own drag again. To make things and to plan ideas, because Vegas is essentially like a day job. I know it's a different nine-to-five but you clock in, you do the face, you do the number, you go home. And so, it afforded me the space to start thinking about the future, and start being like, 'Okay, so if I don't want to be exhausted and sad all the time, what do I want out of this experience?'"

Another benefit for Yvie was the opportunity to build deeper relationships with other Ru girls—to finally experience the benefits of having a sisterhood. "I loved the dressing room. I will never forget how much fun it is to share a dressing room with those girls. It's a different experience than touring, because when we're all touring, even if you're all in the same room, you're all groggy, you all just got off a bus, you all went out last night, you all got fucked up. You're all exhausted and just trying to piece yourself together in the four hours you have before you have to do it again. But with this experience, it was like, 'Oh, how are the wife and kids?' 'Oh my God. Have you heard this Mariah Carey song from 2007?' And I was recently texting Doug about how much I miss being in a room with Derrick Barry, and just getting to hear her 'Derrick Barry' her way through life. She's just so magical."

KiiroKeishi 🅾 @kiirokeishi

Vegas gave Yvie the opportunity to bond with the other cast members and be their true self. It also gave the other cast members the opportunity to get to know Yvie on a much deeper level. Asia shares, "Yvie markets themselves as being weird, and I think I expected them to be a lot more weird than they actually are. I expected them to be sleeping hanging from their feet like Count Dracula, and eating bats, and just being strange. And I've told this to Yvie a hundred times, I call them Yvie Normal instead of Yvie Oddly because I was like, 'You're just like the rest of us.'" Yvie probably cringes that someone referred to them as "normal" but it's accurate. What is "weird" to one person may be completely normal to another. Yvie is less odd than they are different, but Yvie Differently didn't sound like a good name.

After a month of rehearsals, the show opened on January 26, 2020, but in March of that same year, like much of the planet, the show shut down because of the COVID-19 pandemic. The cast and crew were sent home and told to wait it out.

Days turned into weeks, which turned into months. When it was clear that the pandemic was going to last for more than a minute, Yvie and Doug (who had moved from Boston to Las Vegas to be with Yvie during the lockdown) packed everything into a van and headed back to Denver.

In July of 2021, Yvie and the cast got the call that *Drag Race Live* was going to be reopening in August. Yvie—refreshed from a year off—packed up their things and returned to Las Vegas, this time with a different perspective. "*Drag Race* was grueling. But after already doing something so ridiculously hard for me, when I did get back, I was like,

'Okay. I remember this song. Yeah, if I don't have a step, I don't have a step.' So, I enjoyed it, actually, especially because a lot about the experience had changed. I now had the energy and the access to do other things with my life, if I wanted to. And I flourished. I made my first adult friend there in a long-ass time. I had so much great sex. So much bad sex. I mean, I truly loved the Vegas experience. I'm a person who, I realize, focuses a lot on the negative, because that's what colors the things that I do find positive in life. But by the end of the six months I was there, the second time, I was sad to go. I was a little sad to miss that 'coworkers at the office' feeling. But also, I had finally gotten to see some of the gay scene; I had made regular gay friends there. I had started to do things and build little relationships in the city. That's when I realized that you can live anywhere and make it a home."

For Yvie, the Vegas experience came at the right time and gave them exactly what they needed to reconnect with who they were. It gave them the energy they needed to be prepared for the next step. Which happened to be returning to the place where it all began.

YVIE'S TOP 5 FAVORITE
POORLY DRAWN
SEX POSITIONS

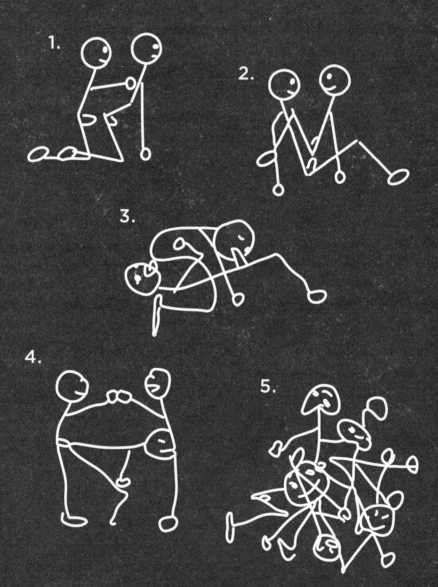

CHAPTER 8

AN INCONVENIENT SEQUEL: THE *ALL STARS, ALL WINNERS* EXPERIENCE

One day in December of 2021, Yvie's phone rang. It was a producer from World of Wonder who explained that they were considering doing a season of *RuPaul's Drag Race All Stars* where all the contestants were previous winners. The rules would be different, and no one would be going home. Yvie's reaction was immediate. "Like, 'Oh my God, yes.' There were plenty of the other girls who got cast, and plenty of other winners, who have said that they had or would have stipulations. But for me, ultimately, I had been in conflict with how I had grown since the show, and what I was fully capable of. How my legacy, for me, was left in such a questionable state, with more to prove. Because at this point, I was still the only person to ever win *Drag Race* with only one maxi-challenge win, aka the worst, aka the least deserving. And then, my drag style also being something that doesn't necessarily refute that. So, there's a lot of the impostor syndrome still in me at this point. But even if this opportunity had never come up, I was still looking for a way to try and prove myself, not only to the people, but I think more so to myself."

We need some clarification here, for the record. Yvie is correct in that, when they won, they had the fewest maxi-challenge wins of any of the winners to date. BeBe Zahara Benet (winner, season 1), Jinkx Monsoon (winner, season 5), and Sasha Velour (winner, season 9) each had two maxi-challenge wins, and all the others had three wins, excluding Sharon Needles (winner, season 4), who had four wins. However, Willow Pill (winner, season 14 and Yvie's drag daughter) only had one maxi-challenge win and was in the bottom twice, compared to Yvie's one time in the bottom. When you include *All Stars*, the maxi-challenge win-to-winner ratio is very different. Monét X Change (cowinner, *All Stars,* season 4) only had one maxi-challenge win and was in the bottom twice. Kylie Sonique Love (winner, *All Stars,* season 6) only had one win and was in the bottom three times. And Trixie Mattel (winner, *All Stars,* season 3) never won a maxi-challenge and was in the bottom twice. These are important statistics in determining who the "worst" winners and the "best" winners are. What matters is that Yvie won. But that logic also doesn't take away Yvie's feelings.

"When they called with the opportunity, I thought it would be a way for me to be portrayed in a different light, and to show all the skills that I have been passionate about refining and working on. And also to get the opportunity to do things I never did on *Drag Race,* because there were a number of challenges I would have liked to have done on season 11, but just never got to because there's only so many episodes. It's all of these things combined, plus the fact that I had already been in this weird creative rush that I always get around November-December, when the gigs slow down, the weather gets cold, we're all snowed in. So that, on top of the fact that we were still in the grips of a pandemic and I wasn't working the most, I was creating so much. I had already been dreaming so much. I had gotten to this point where I couldn't even sleep all night. I'd wake up in the middle of these very abstract dreams of floating dresses, and shapes, and measuring tape, and like, 'Can you make a this out of a that?'

"Ultimately, it just felt like everything had come together, especially because the fans, myself included, had always wanted to see a winner's season. But it was never going to be possible with how busy all of the winners were. Yet here we were, still all kind of locked in with time on our hands, and I think each of us had something to prove. It was a yes from the start. But I also assumed they were going to pay us more money than the first time, because we're winners, we have no legitimate reason to do this. That's the thing: It's awesome to go back on *Drag Race* because it's the biggest platform for the craft. But we have no real reason to compete anymore. And that's something that you already see on regular

All Stars seasons—the girls juggling whether or not they want this second crown, even if it ruins a friendship."

Yvie's comments track. It's been reported that contestants on *Drag Race* make four hundred dollars per episode but receive a five percent increase for subsequent seasons. That means contestants on previous seasons of *All Stars* received four hundred twenty dollars per episode. That's a far cry from what a popular queen could be making on tour. To put it in perspective, however, contestants on *Big Brother* earn one thousand dollars per week of filming, yet the lovelorn contestants on *The Bachelor* don't get paid at all. That said, it's been rumored that for the ninth installment of *All Stars*, the queens have been paid a performance fee of fifty thousand dollars each, with an additional twenty-five thousand for outfits. Obviously, WOW is recognizing that if you want your stars back, you have to pay them.

Yvie's reaction to the invite may have been an immediate yes, but they still questioned that decision as they got ready to film. The driving force behind agreeing to appear was a desire to prove they deserved to win season 11—to combat their imposter syndrome—because whether or not it's true (and it's not), they believe many people don't think they should have won. But that could be said about any winner. Some people will be happy their favorite queen wins, and some people will not. Someone has to win, which means someone has to lose.

But Yvie was also concerned about whether or not they wanted to go through another emotional experience of competing in a reality television show. Season 11 had a serious emotional impact on Yvie, and they weren't sure if another round was going to be better or worse.

Ultimately, they saw *All Stars, All Winners* as a Rudemption. "Of course, part of me was still focused on trying to be the best drag queen I could be, and standing out in the pack, and reinforcing why they crowned me in the first place. And it would be fantastic to have won and to have been better accepted in the competition. But more than anything, I really wanted to have fun, because during season 11, even though there were moments where I got to bond with the girls, and moments where we would laugh and kiki, so much of the experience, especially in the Werk Room when the cameras were on, was the tension between me still wanting to have fun and be one of the girls, but also me not being there for the bullshit. So, coming back offered every opportunity to try things in a different light."

The official offer to appear came in January 2022 and Yvie immediately accepted. Unlike season 11, where Yvie had two and a half weeks to prepare, this time they had two and a half months to get ready. That changed Yvie's game. "I was feeling confident. Especially since a few of the runways could be fulfilled by the ideas that I'd already been working on. I was working on this yarn jacket, pantsuit-thingy combo because I had a bunch of crochet swim-wear cover-ups and a bunch of yarn just sitting around my house. And to get a knitting category, I was like, 'Well, that's perfect. One dream down.' So, it was a pretty easy process throwing out the ideas I wanted, and also knowing how I wanted to tackle this. I really wanted to pay tribute to the Yvie who had to craft everything on season 11. And also, to show how I've grown, because I can sew now. That is definitely not something I could do on season 11. And I wanted to show people how Yvie the human being dresses on a runway. I think a month later they gave us an updated list along with the list of lip-sync songs. And that was the first point where I kind of got a sense that maybe this season wasn't going to be for me."

As time for preparation went on, the producers started to change their minds—which they do and have the right to do. Creating a reality television show is like building a plane while it's flying. When WOW sent Yvie the first list, they may not have had the entire cast signed. New cast members may have meant changes were required. But those changes started to shift Yvie's perspective and cause concern that maybe this wasn't going to be the Rudemption they were looking for. "I think it was the ball that came in the updated list. We had already had a Dolly Parton runway, so already I'm being required to push way outside of my comfort zone. And then we get a *Wheel of Fortune* Ball—everybody is familiar with *Wheel of Fortune*—which wasn't ever something where I thought, 'Yes! I need to make drag about *Wheel of Fortune*. That is what speaks to my soul.' So, when the second category was a Vanna White runway, I was like, 'Are you guys kidding me? We already have one blonde woman on the runway. I am not going to pour my heart and soul into another blonde woman, dragging myself up for her.' Especially since it really doesn't get better than Dolly Parton. She might not be *my* drag, but that bitch *is* drag.

"And then with the lip-syncs, the initial list they gave us included a lot of the songs that we ended up getting, but it was almost entirely older songs. They had one song from a newer generation, and that was Lizzo's "Better in Color," which I was so excited about because I already had ideas to perform that as it was. So, I was like, 'Okay, so maybe they're kind of tossing me a bone here and giving me one song that you can dance to.' The rest of them were all older, specifically with two or three of them being older musical theater or cabaret numbers. When I got those, I thought, 'They really want Jinkx or Monét to win.' I know the rest of us can do these songs and would kill these songs, but Ella Fitzgerald's 'Old McDonald' and 'The Night the Lights Went Out in Georgia' spoken word from *Designing Women*?

"What ended up being a major point of contention later in the season was 'The Ladies Who Lunch' from Stephen Sondheim's *Company*. That song was made for Jinkx. And she would've been amazing in it, but it got pulled because the rest of the cast complained. I saw those three and a slew of other old, outdated B sides and I was like, 'Oh, I'm just here to be here.' And I started putting all my effort into trying to find creative ways to win these lip-syncs because I was still like, 'You know what? They're going to give me a shot. They know I'm a good lip-syncer, so I want to prove that I can do it to all these different things, in all these different styles.' Because that's something else people didn't really get to see from me on my season. But I still feel like I deluded myself back into the fantasy of being taken seriously."

It's also important to understand that television shows can't just play a song. World of Wonder must have permission to air each song. So, while they were able to air "Supernova" by Kylie

Minogue and "Kings & Queens" by Ava Max, maybe they couldn't get permission to use "Hold Up" by Beyoncé and had to settle for "Green Light." The workings of television are complex and involve a lot of lawyers.

Yet Yvie's comments highlight an innate challenge in the concept behind *All Stars, All Winners*: creating a show where you can give every queen the opportunity to shine. A perfect song for Yvie would potentially be very different from the perfect song for The Vivienne, or Raja.

Looking back at the *All Stars, All Winners* cast, there are eight very different queens, with eight very different styles and skill sets. It's one thing to put together a cast of *Drag Race* where the queens need to adapt to the challenges—most will happily do so because they want to win. We've seen instances where the queens feel their brand is so well defined that they don't show enough range on the show, and they ultimately go home. *All Stars* is similar in that the queens have an opportunity at a second chance, and while they are able to bring their own style to each challenge, they still must and do adapt. *All Stars, All Winners* brought together eight superstar queens who had won their respective seasons, all of whom have very defined styles of drag. Making them conform to challenges is like pushing a square peg through a round hole.

As Yvie prepared to head back to the studio, they were already starting to feel uncomfortable. In season 11, they started filming while exhausted and overwhelmed, but at least they felt that they were a contender. For *All Stars, All Winners*, they started filming feeling confident, but like they might be an infamous "filler queen." They didn't feel like there was going to be a storyline where they could be seen as a contender for the crown. Maybe that was some of their old narratives resurfacing (hello, imposter syndrome, my old friend), but it was still shaping their outlook.

Yet Yvie didn't let that deter them. They were determined to show the world how they had grown since season 11. "The beginning of *All Stars*, as much as I still wanted to prove myself, was not in the same way that I wanted to prove myself on season 11. On season 11, I already knew that my runways would be iconic, but I knew I needed to prove myself in every single challenge that came at me. Not as much for the fans, but so that I could be better in the competition, so that I'd win more. And this time coming in, I just wanted to prove how much I enjoy drag, and I wanted to prove I'm capable of carrying that into all these challenges they throw at us. And just give people the authentic Yvie that I feel so comfortable doing outside of television. When I came in, I was thinking, 'This is going to be a wild ride, it's going to be fun. I'm going to get to have a completely different experience.' From the way they sold it to us, it sounded like they were going to do everything in their power not to make me feel like a fool. 'Nobody's going home, we're going to have lots of challenges to try and test out all these different facets of your drag and your capability. And it's going to be a big old, gay old time because you guys are all our legends and icons.'"

From Yvie's perspective, the producers tried to make *All Stars, All Winners* a different experience. "I think they did the best they could with pulling together what they got, and out of what

Hannah Chusid ⬡ @hannahsgothhaus

they gave. When we arrived, it felt like they had made a number of miscalculations, especially by the end of the first challenge or two, at how clear they were with their intentions with this show, and how that was not expressed to almost any of the competitors. And I really don't want to sound like a bitter bitch, but they very, very clearly were taking care of Jinkx in a different way."

This may be an inconvenient truth, but it doesn't surprise. In watching *All Stars, All Winners*, it's easy to suspect that the show was being shaped around Jinkx Monsoon. That's not to say that Jinkx doesn't have the skills. Jinkx, the winner of season 5, is an amazing talent with seemingly endless potential. But this is a reality television show, meaning there's little "real" about it. The content may be unscripted, but that doesn't mean the producers don't have a hand in shaping how things play out. That's not to say that World of Wonder had predetermined the winner. It is to say that the final cut of the episodes *seemed* to be slanted toward Jinkx. And perhaps that comes down to casting. Looking across the eight contestants, Jinkx is one of the most successful queens to ever set foot on the *Drag Race* set—along with the likes of Bianca Del Rio and Trixie Mattel. Meaning no disrespect to any of the *All Stars, All Winners* contestants or to discount their achievements, but Jinkx is the only one to have done a sold-out run of *Chicago* on Broadway, as but one example.

Yvie shares, "Before they let us out of our hotel rooms, we were all able to negotiate for different concessions we needed in their very strict rules; for our mental health, or for our business or whatever. It became this dynamic of what we all wanted, and what we as the winners coming back to this experience were told that we were going to get, to be shown in a positive light. And then there was what Jinkx had. It felt like she had a different contract. I was very frustrated, because as an example, I had to fight to have them let me smoke pot, since I don't take any other pain meds. I was like, 'You guys, we're in a state where it's legal and you won't let me manage my pain in the one way I do, when you guys are more than down to feed us drinks on set?'"

It is entirely possible that Jinkx had a different contract. And there's nothing wrong with that. It happens all the time where one person negotiates a better deal than another person doing the exact same job. Take Ellen Pompeo, for example, who plays the title character on the show *Grey's Anatomy* (and who was a judge on *All Stars,* season 4, episode 8). In the initial seasons of the show, her costar Patrick Dempsey was reportedly paid more, even though Pompeo was the show's main character. So maybe Jinkx's people negotiated a different contract.

That isn't to say that Jinkx didn't deserve to win. As Yvie explains, "Going in, especially once we finally got the confirmation, and saw all the bitches in the room, I was like, 'Okay, this is going to be Jinkx's competition. She is going to be the one to beat.' But I thought that doing the show was an opportunity to show how I had evolved."

Things on the set of *All Stars, All Winners* were fluid, for lack of a better word, because they had eight unique queens and they wanted to highlight all of them. In a regular season, producers start filming with a clear idea of the challenges, largely because they're dealing with contestants they can control. *All Stars, All Winners* was *not* a regular season.

Even feeling like they didn't have the chance to win, one of the main things that bothered Yvie was a feeling that the judges didn't know who Yvie was, who Yvie had evolved into. Yvie says that the judges were critical of them, suggesting to Yvie that they didn't know who they are as an artist. Viewers didn't get to see that because it all ended up on the cutting room floor. The producers chose to show a narrative that focused only on the positive reactions of the judges, which was obvious to the fans. The judging was a love-in and nary a bad word was said.

Whether accurate or not, Yvie didn't feel the producers considered them as valuable as some of the other contestants. "I'm supposed to be judged as a legend, as somebody who has already made their impact. And yet these people clearly do not know what I am about and what I've done since the show, and don't see me as my own standout artist. I saw this specifically with me, Jaida, and The Vivienne the most; the people who I assume the judges have had the least interaction with since our seasons. And so, they did the same thing with us that they do with all the girls who come into *Drag Race* for the first time, ignoring and devaluing all the things that the judges don't understand or relate to. You're still going to get the same critique next week if you don't fix something, and this time it's actually going to mean something. It's frustrating because going back, I didn't think I was still going to be judged like I need to learn about who Yvie is, like I needed to learn how to market myself to my audience that I had built."

All in all, Yvie didn't love the experience of filming *All Stars, All Winners*. There were moments when they felt they were being successful, but so many moments that were reinforcing their imposter syndrome. As Yvie's husband, Doug, explains, "When Yvie came back from filming, they were really down. They were down on how it was going to be perceived. They talked about how some fans would be like, 'Yvie is the worst winner statistically.' And then Yvie was like, 'Well now I just went on the show and proved that.' I would have to snap them out of it and say, 'That is fucking wild to say, and it's not real.' And it's not an overwhelming thing, but it's definitely there in the back of their head. The producers didn't show the judges telling Yvie that they didn't know themself, which is just one of the most ridiculous critiques they could have. Yvie is one of the people who stays most true to themselves in their drag. But that was one of the critiques they got, and it was just not a great experience. And then watching it back, being all whitewashed where there was no negative feedback, it was weird. And I'd be like, 'Oh my God, look at all this positive feedback you're getting from the fans about this outfit, or this performance or whatever.' But I think they were just really excited for it to be over, and I kind of was too."

There were moments when Yvie felt that—while they weren't likely to win—they were at least going to achieve their goal of showing the fans that they deserved to be a winner. One of those moments was the Big Bad Wolf (episode 4, "Fairytale Justice"), where they created one of the funniest, most iconic characters the show has ever seen. They held their own against powerhouse

Alina Britschgi @alinab.art

comedians like Jinkx and The Vivienne, and they had fun doing it. "It was the first time in the competition, since stepping through the doors and seeing that shit was going to be different than I thought, that I felt like I was really being successful. That I felt like I did so many times on season 11 where I was like, 'Oh, I am a real contender.' And not even in the context of the competition, but while I was performing as the Big Bad Wolf, I felt like myself, instead of thinking about whether or not this is going to impress the judges. Because by this point, I had already lost all hope and I actually just had fun. I felt like I was in improv class in high school. There was that, combined with the fact that this was the first runway that I didn't personally make all myself. I was like, 'Okay, this is exactly what the judges are looking for. It's going to be my fashion moment. It's going to be my funny moment.' That week I felt taken seriously. And one of the girls even brought my name up as an afterthought of who might win, which was really, really big at this point in the competition. They were like, 'Yeah, I think it's going to be Jinkx and Vivienne. Oh, but Yvie, you were really great this week too.' So, I was like, 'Oh my God. You guys, it could be me.'"

Even Snatch Game was a proud moment for Yvie. Well, maybe not proud, but not the worst. Not that they enjoyed it—Snatch Game remains a sore spot—but they didn't hate it as much because they knew they weren't going home, which reduced their stress. "One of the original two choices I was going in with was Rico Nasty. And I did something that I didn't ever think I would be able to do—make RuPaul laugh. But I chose her because I finally saw my representation somewhere in mainstream pop culture, this alt rock, rap screamer, bad bitch energy who resonates with plenty of the kids. And that's an impersonation I can do, and also flex my freestyle muscles on. So I was going in with her and I was going in with Tim Gunn, who I was nervous about because he's a more muted character, even though I think that leads to other comedic opportunities. What if I was going to be there with, say, Jinkx Monsoon as Judy Garland? How would you even speak up if something like that were to happen? Other than be like, 'Oh, Judy, I love that song. You made it work, designer.' It wasn't a strong character. And then I don't even know what it was that got me thinking about the Boogey Man, but I was like, 'What if I did the Boogey Man as the Boog*ie* Man? Like he's a dancing demon?' And I started playing with his voice around the house, and it was making my friends laugh so I was like, 'Okay, we're going with this direction. Tim Gunn, you're a backup.'

Ultimately for Yvie, Snatch Game was a little less horrible on *All Stars, All Winners* than it was on their original season. Why? As Yvie explains, "I think it's because I was getting something back from Ru. From the walk-through on season 11, I knew that Ru was going to hate Whoopi. And it was very different to have Ru be responsive to that character at all. So, I was like, 'Oh, okay then. I don't have to try to be funny. I don't have to try and hit into your sense of humor.' I still went into Snatch Game knowing it was going to be my weakest week because I don't think I have the sense of humor to relate to Ru in those situations. And add in the extra challenge of doing impersonations, because I don't do well as 'other people.' Even if it's an exaggeration, I just don't like being confined to a character. I'd like to build the character myself. And even then, I still really did not make RuPaul laugh as the Boogie Man. She chuckled once or twice, but her big takeaway from that, like everyone, was, 'Wow, you're sexy.' So, that's a positive thing."

In rewatching *All Stars, All Winners*, it's clear that a key ingredient was missing from Yvie's sparkle. "There was no fire. And that's what the producers had the hardest time trying to get out of me. By that point, all the fucking joy that I was trying to fake and inject into it was gone. But I stayed. I stayed through everything because I was desperate for people to get to see a different side of me. I was desperately hopeful that maybe they'd give me a thought. And by the time we finished filming everything, I was just desperately hopeful that the producers would do their best to at least make it look like I was there, or like I ever had a chance of even being a runner-up."

Regardless of what happened, *All Stars, All Winners* had one thing going for it that the producers couldn't take away from Yvie: a room full of friends. "Instead of having to wrestle with being camera shy or nervous, there was this general sense of knowing that we're all here to try and win, to try and be the queen of all queens. But also, to put on a TV show. So, there's really not a whole lot of interpersonal drama that can pop up, because it's the same feeling we all get when we're in a bar or at a pride event and there's another queen booked there with us. Where it's like, 'Oh my God, I loved you on your season. It's so cool to get to see you in person. I'm very excited to see what you're going to work with.' And some light, casual shade."

It may not have been the Rudemption that Yvie had hoped for, but in the end, *All Stars, All Winners* provided Yvie with an opportunity to show the *Drag Race* fandom how they had elevated their drag, and that they did, in fact, deserve the crown.

YVIE'S TOP 5 FICTIONAL FUCKS

1. The DNA guy from *Jurassic Park*

2. Jack Skellington

3. The gargoyles from the show *Gargoyles*

4. The gargoyles from *The Hunchback of Notre Dame*

5. All of the X-Men

CHAPTER 9

A FANATIC HEART: YVIE AND THEIR FANS

Yvie has a complex relationship with their fans. And that is commonly referred to as a "massive understatement." It's fair to say that when Yvie was auditioning for *Drag Race*, they didn't have a realistic expectation of what would happen after they were announced as a cast member on season 11. Their objective was to have a platform to share their art. But the fans had other ideas. And a reminder here about the language warning from the beginning of the book. Because you're about to read some words . . .

"By the time we were halfway through season 11, I was already exhausted by the fandom. While you're airing, you will have the most people in your ears in the most places, whether or not you asked for it, telling you, 'I love you. I hate you. Go die, nigger.' All of it is so overwhelming. But also having to deal with the public expectations and the public love, and not being able to just go down the street and eat some ice cream without having somebody tell you how much you've changed their life. I don't think the human ego needs as much attention and stroking in positive or negative ways as it gets when you're on *Drag Race*."

By the time Yvie was crowned the winner of season 11, they were working harder than they ever had in their life, on top of living with a chronic illness (hEDS) that left them in constant pain. Winning only turned the pressure up, and they didn't have a moment to relax and process all of the emotions they were experiencing. The beast of celebrity needed feeding. "After I won, I had given up on trying to please people because, for me, *Drag Race* was the big finale of what I can give. I gave you the best I will ever do in my life, and I'm exhausted now, and I need a minute to figure out who I am, and what I want, and where to go."

Perhaps something that has made the circumstances worse is interactions with and responses from other queens, the most famous of which was a Twitter exchange with Bianca del Rio (winner, season 6), which Yvie has dubbed "Chef Gate." Yvie was in a bad place and took to Twitter as a way to express how they were feeling. Bianca responded in true Bianca fashion. For all the talk about Ru girls being part of a sisterhood, there has been a lot of shade thrown around.

A Fanatic Heart: Yvie and Their Fans

 Yvie Oddly (blue checkmark) @OddlyYvie · Jul 21, 2019 ···
Imagine that you're a very passionate chef who just landed your dream job at a prestigious restaurant. Imagine that you just spent a long day on your feet cooking for people who pay you because they appreciate how your food tastes.

 Bianca Del Rio @TheBiancaDelRio · Jul 21, 2019 ···
It's only been a FEW MONTHS..... GOOD LUCK BITCH! 😳😳😳😳

 Yvie Oddly (blue checkmark) @OddlyYvie · Jul 21, 2019 ···
Which is why I put this out here now. I don't care how anyone else deals with "fame" but I have very real boundaries so if I have to be a bitch who sets the precedent of reminding people we are humans then so be it.

 Bianca Del Rio @TheBiancaDelRio · Jul 21, 2019 ···
Like I said.... GOOD LUCK! 🐨

 Yvie Oddly (blue checkmark) @OddlyYvie · Jul 21, 2019 ···
I don't need luck. I've got the nerve to do things on my own terms...which is apparently uncommon

 Bianca Del Rio @TheBiancaDelRio · Jul 21, 2019 ···
After reading these tweets, I can agree you do have A LOT OF NERVE. 👍🌀

 Yvie Oddly (blue checkmark) @OddlyYvie · Jul 21, 2019 ···
Someone has to. The last queen who had this much nerve now wastes it trolling twitter

 Bianca Del Rio @TheBiancaDelRio · Jul 21, 2019 ···
I wish I could troll more, but a fan just asked me for a picture.... BE RIGHT BACK! 😃

"Where my relationship really fractured with the fans was Chef Gate, with me going into a very long and angry metaphorical-laden rant after I told a bunch of fans no to a photo in the middle of an exhausting tour. And then they followed me and all the girls back to the hotel and tried to take photos at the hotel, and then got into an argument with me when I told them that no means no. So I was fueled up by how inhuman I felt, by how little control I'd had in my life, how little of a voice I'd had. And I went on Twitter, knowing how much influence and how many eyeballs were still on me, to be like, 'Leave me the fuck alone. I know people love me, but I clearly do not want the attention right now.'"

A phenomenon that has developed in the age of social media is the toxic belief among some fans that celebrities are their property. The bigger the queen, the worse it is. The topic is triggering for Yvie. "People can say forever and ever, 'You know what you signed up for when you went on *Drag Race*.' That is the most rapey bullshit you can say about celebrities—that they know what they signed up for. That does not make the parts about the culture that aren't right, right. And maybe the issue is I was naive enough to think that I could, in any way, with the influence I had garnered, get people to change their fucking perspective, kill their idols, and see me as a real person, especially when I just did twenty backflips in twenty different cities. I'm hobbling outside of a show, and you're going to give me fucking sass because you think I think I'm too good to take a picture with my lowly fans who got me here when you did not fucking get me here. Your support gives me opportunities, but if you don't support me as a human, you can't

Lady Ava Garland Kensington

support me as an artist, and that's what I needed to scream out to the people, but maybe not using the best words.

"I needed them to see how angry and frustrated I was. Especially because for the few years that followed, especially after the noise died down a little bit, people did see that. And it sounds sick to say this, but people were nervous about bugging me for a photo because they fucking should be. Because I am a human being, because what other person would you feel comfortable walking up to in the middle of a dinner with their grandparents and being like, 'Oh my God, I thought Brooke Lynn should have won. But I have to say, I watched it back and I loved you.' What other person do you just run up to in real life and interrupt them while knowing that you're not showing them any courtesy or acknowledging their humanity? The sickest part for me is when people will run up, especially when I'm clearly trying to hide, trying to relax, and they'll be like, 'Oh, I know this must be so annoying, but can you take a picture for me?' Honestly, I'm more annoyed by the fact that they know that it's annoying, and that they say they know that it's annoying, and then they still would do it. If you know that you're infringing upon my time, freedom, peace of mind, at least have the common courtesy to not outwardly be like, 'Yep, I'm making you feel uncomfortable. Will you do this for me anyways?' If you're going to be that fucking rude, just go all the way so that we don't have to pretend like I'm a human for a second, okay? Because that's what's annoying."

Considering the situation, it's not a surprise that Yvie would be emotional when talking about this. For all the love they receive from the fans, they receive an equal amount of hate (if not more). A Twitter search of "Yvie Oddly hate" proves the point.

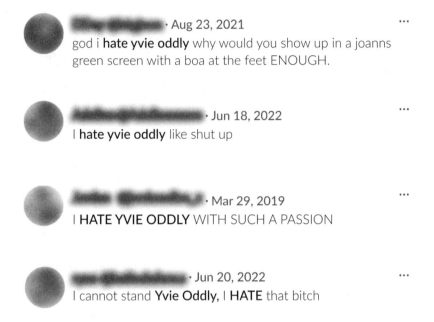

god i **hate yvie oddly** why would you show up in a joanns green screen with a boa at the feet ENOUGH.

· Aug 23, 2021 ···

I **hate yvie oddly** like shut up

· Jun 18, 2022 ···

I **HATE YVIE ODDLY** WITH SUCH A PASSION

· Mar 29, 2019 ···

I cannot stand **Yvie Oddly, I HATE** that bitch

· Jun 20, 2022 ···

While the names and faces have been removed to protect the guilty, the point is clear. The internet gives people permission to be their worst selves. They feel completely justified putting messages out into the world that, if challenged, they wouldn't dare say to a person's face. It's easy for someone on Twitter to say, "I cannot stand Yvie Oddly, I HATE that bitch," but they clearly aren't someone who has ever had to face the wrath of the world. They can hide behind a social media account where no one really knows who they are. Some fans appear to have no sense that they are publicly attacking human beings and have no empathy for them. Worse still are the moments where other queens who have experienced the *Drag Race* phenomenon do things that are not supportive of one another. Those actions can lead to some seriously bad situations and unresolved moments.

One of those moments came from *Drag Race* alums Katya Zamolodchikova (known simply as Katya) and Trixie Mattel, which frankly comes across as a little personal. Katya and Trixie went so far as to publish comments in their book *Trixie and Katya's Guide to Modern Womanhood* that directly attacked Yvie. The specifics of the passage in the book are about Yvie's look at DragCon NYC in 2019. Their outfit included a white T-shirt dress with a fake price tag indicating it cost "$100k" with green puffy-paint letters that read "Really Expensive Fashion." Yvie wore smudged lipstick and eyeshadow, with a red pentagram on their head. The look was meant to be a statement about socioeconomics, the fans' response to them having won *Drag Race*, and the expectation that Yvie's looks should suddenly be more elevated.

It's not so much that Katya and Trixie said what they said. It's that they put those words in a book that became a *New York Times* bestseller and has been read by thousands of people. A tweet is one thing, but a book is something considerably more permanent. And bearing in mind Katya's struggles on *Drag Race*, one might expect that they would be more sensitive and aware of the potential ramifications.

Yvie says, "In the year that I was still reigning and still fighting the hardest accusations, allegations, and hateful shit from the fans, Katya and Trixie had a book where they, for some reason, kept in a whole passage calling me lazy, saying because my DragCon looks weren't like Violet Chachki's . . . Katya was like, 'You're a winner and you look like you don't give a fuck about anything.'"

Yvie is paraphrasing. What the excerpt actually said was "Represent the brand! Carry the torch for a year! But if you're firmly established with an aesthetic, all you've got to do is polish up a little bit or present your best self. The bar is raised. But she went the other direction, and it seemed like she was trolling. And on one level I don't care, because doing drag in itself is trolling. But on the other hand, you just look like a side of guacamole with lashes. You look like whodunnit and run. You know what I mean?"

Yvie continues, "I was frustrated because she could see the outcome. And one of my favorite chaos trash artists could see the end effect I was going for, that I didn't want to look like I gave a shit about DragCon. That I looked like 'fuck this whole ideal and this whole mess.' And then Katya sided with the machine and was like, 'Why did you look cheap? You cheap, ugly bitch.'

"And I'm like, 'Because this whole piece was about how I don't have resources, I don't have energy, and I don't have the fandom on my side.' I have people expecting, for some reason, this weird pattern that Ru girls had started going into: get on the show, immediately become beautiful, and always wear garments worth thousands of dollars, when I still did not have that kind of money. I put everything I had into that show and into maintaining my drag."

Yvie isn't losing sleep over the moment with Katya and Trixie, or anyone else for that matter. But those moments remain present in their mind, even if only in the deep crevices. Meaning, they're keeping a list. "I'm not particularly holding on to a lot. But I still remember everything that every queen said about me at all the important junctures in my life. And I still have a little list when I come across girls where I'm like, 'Are you going to say anything about the fact that you stoked the fire for the fandom?'"

In these moments, Yvie is being true to Yvie, and the Yvie that the world saw on season 11 of *Drag Race*. They're not putting up with people who aren't honest. When the infamous Chef Gate Twitter exchange occurred with Bianca, a number of other queens piled on, making claims that they would never treat their fans the way Yvie had, but from Yvie's perspective, that wasn't truthful. "I'm still in the same dressing rooms with all these drag queens who are all looking for escape routes from the venue to avoid the fans. We'll have security so that we don't have to talk to anybody and have people who we literally pay to lie for us and be like, 'Oh, sorry, no selfies allowed. Oh, she's got a flight to catch.'"

The situation with Bianca was a little different, however. "It was frustrating for me that somebody with that much influence, and that much power, and that much say and sway in the communal mindset and perception of drag queens, was punching down. So I was pissed at her, especially because she then talked about me in interviews. And I had been, not avoiding, but very thankful that our schedules had never lined up. Then she came to the Vegas show while I was performing. And that's what really changed things, because the thing that she did, that so many other people on my list have never done, was acknowledge the tension, acknowledge the time when she talked down about a drag queen who was just learning how to be famous and clearly does not like the way she's being treated. And she didn't say, 'I'm sorry.' She didn't say, 'It was so wrong of me.' She just said, 'Can I have a photo?' And then in that joke also told me, 'I was just fucking around. I have respect for you.'"

For Yvie, things with the fans have improved somewhat, largely because Yvie now has a better sense of who they are, and what they can and cannot give. "I am no longer in a place where I feel like I have no space, and no time, and no me for myself. So I can indulge somebody's selfishness, and I can indulge somebody's want to take a picture with this superstar that they never thought existed out in the world. And that's changed a lot, but I think what's also changed is I just see how people treat and feel about famous people. Despite me shouting into the void, it's so hard to change that perception. I'm trying to do it in more casual ways than I was before. I'll openly bitch to literally anyone and everyone about how I don't like being treated like a piece of meat. How I don't like that the public perception of me is always going to come from one TV show, despite the fact that I have lived and will live a lot more life. I'll let people know that I don't like being fangirled while they're fangirling me. But I also acknowledge and address how weird it is to see a superstar. I'm just trying to help people kill their idols more gently. Be like, 'I saw Yvie Oddly, she took a picture with me, it was really cool. She was exhausted, and she said she hated doing drag that day. She said that she wanted to go out and suck some dick instead.'"

Yvie is *not* advocating *killing* anyone. More that people should stop idolizing people in an unhealthy manner, and should treat celebrities as human beings, deserving of privacy and personal space. In this climate, it felt like that needed to be clarified.

Yvie's relationship with the fans has improved, but it's still complicated, largely because Yvie struggles to put themself in the position of the fan. They have idols, but how they would interact with those idols is very different from most. "I would never do a meet and greet. I'm hard-pressed to go to live shows of artists that I like because I like my personal experiences with their music, or their art, or whatever. But I don't think, no matter how high I have anyone on a pedestal, that I would ever pay for an experience that is as—I don't want to say fake, but constructed—as man-made as a meet and greet. Maybe it's because I've seen the other side of it for so long, even before *Drag Race*. Having to be at meet and greets with the other Ru girls, I don't think I'd ever want to pay for an experience where somebody has to kiss my ass like that."

In some ways, Yvie is the antihero of superstars. They want to interact with their fans, and their idols, in a way that is humanizing, and real. "I personally would want to bump into someone like Beyoncé on the street. But I wouldn't want to start our interaction off with, 'Oh my God, I'm such a big fan.' In an ideal world, I want to be able to have something to talk about with Beyoncé, like, 'Oh my God, you like soup? I like soup. What a coincidence. What's your favorite type of soup?' Something to deconstruct. And if you need to get out your fangirlness, because we all do, then you say, 'I love soup, it's amazing. And I just want to say it's mind-blowing to meet you. Can't believe I got to see you eating soup.' Leave the interaction."

Like everything in life, Yvie isn't consistent about how a fan interaction should go. It will depend on a multitude of factors, none of
which can be predicted. It's really an experiment. Yvie doesn't know
what they want in that moment, and the fan doesn't know either.
The advice is simply to have fun. And bring some soup.

YVIE'S TOP 5 FAVORITE PLACES TO GET NAKED

1. The park

2. The beach

3. Anywhere outside

4. Anywhere inside

5. Your place

CHAPTER 10

LOVE OF MY LOVES: YVIE ON RELATIONSHIPS

Relationships are hard at the best of times. Anyone who's ever been in a relationship knows that. But it takes on a different complexity when you add in LGBTQIA+ identities. Yvie's love life gets even more complicated when you add in intersections of their multiple identities, and eventually their celebrity status.

As a teenager, when Yvie started dating people, they had a sense of being an outcast. "I had a number of girlfriends growing up. But I always had this lingering feeling of 'I'm the leftovers,' and my girlfriends were the leftovers. We were like, 'Oh yeah, we're not popular, or cool, or pretty, or rich. So of course, we should date.' I had this bitter mindset of, 'Damn, I'm always going to be the leftovers.' But what changed for me with that was going to Denver East High School, to the 'regular' school. There were fewer gay people, but for me, it felt more diverse in general, but definitely also in gay life. That's where I first had crushes on guys that weren't unrequited. I was in a little love triangle with two boys in the theater department. One of them was younger than me, and one of them was older. And it was so dramatic because both of them liked me, but neither of them really liked each other. I ended up choosing one, and he was my first boyfriend ever."

That was where Yvie started to tackle some of their internalized homophobia. "At Denver East I started fully tapping into the peacocking. This was the place where I wore the crop tops, and booty shorts, and started wearing makeup to school, and maybe even painted my nails sometimes. Pierced my ears, pierced everything I could pierce. I wanted to show more. So that's where, for some strange reason, I started breaking down at least some of the internalized homophobia."

As a young adult, Yvie kept drag as their dirty little secret out of fear they would be rejected. As Yvie explains, wigs, heels, and dresses "are all the things you still have to hide if you can finally get a guy from Grindr to not ghost you. I'm a gorgeous twink, but I'm still Black in the whitest of white bread cities. I still felt like an outsider."

Relationships and sex took a bit of a back seat for Yvie as they threw themselves more and more into their drag. But at some point, fate intervened. "I met my first real adult boyfriend—Andrew—on

Grindr a few weeks before I would start doing the competition that would rocket me into Denver success." Yvie is referring to competing in Track's Ultimate Queen in 2015. But there was a tiny secret they were keeping from Andrew: the drag thing.

"I would tell guys I was an artist. I'd show them pictures of my paintings, and this and that. But the few times I did tell guys I was a drag queen it was like, 'Oh well, there's the end of the conversation.' It was still very unsexy to do drag as a gay man. So, I really didn't tell guys I did drag. And when I met Andrew, I didn't tell him I was a drag queen. I was like, 'Yeah, I work at Tracks, it's a gay club. I'm an artist. Here's some paintings.' The usual Grindr fluff. And it wasn't until we started getting serious that I was like, 'Okay, so I have to come out to you. I'm also a drag queen, and I'm going to be doing this competition every week. And I'm really good, I promise. And I might win.' He was a scholar, getting ready to go to school for electrochemical engineering or some shit and was like, 'It's so interesting to me that you're doing such a different thing than me in life. And I'm so passionate, and I'll support you.' That was my first relationship with somebody who saw through the drag and didn't care, but also because he wasn't the stereotypical gay. He was a dorky guy who had all straight friends, didn't really go out to the clubs, definitely didn't go to the bathhouses. So in that way, for the first time in my life, it brought me some sense of normalcy and peace. It was like, 'Oh, I have this nice normal boyfriend with a nice normal job. And we go out on nice normal dinners, and he loves me despite the fact that I'm a little bit weird. But I'm never going to be too weird around him or his really normal friends and family.'"

What Yvie was doing is called "editing." That's where you take a piece of your identity and hide it away from your respective other. It's pretty common. Most people do it, particularly when they're young, and very much at the beginning of a new relationship, because we don't have the confidence to show people all of who we are.

"That took years for me to really understand. He was the sweetest guy ever, and he loved so much about me. But there's also so much about me that he never would have been able to handle completely. I was working at the club. I was always partying and drinking. I've never been a good communicator, but in this case, I was living two separate lives. It wasn't a full, mature relationship because I was still separating parts of who I was."

That all changed about six months before *Drag Race* aired. "It was a late night on Grindr, and I had just been announced on *Drag Race*. So, for the first time in my life I was getting the payoff from *Drag Race* that was being deprived from my drag experience before, which is being able to be a sexual human being. And yeah, for the first time in my life there was also a lot of people being like, 'Oh my God, I'm so excited for you. Let's go, Denver.' At least, there were plenty of people who were like, 'I'm so excited for you. Let me suck your dick.' The first guy I hooked up with post-announcement was a Silky fan who told me so after I fucked him. And once I looked around in his apartment, I saw pictures of him with Carson Kressley, and Michelle Visage, and at other meet and

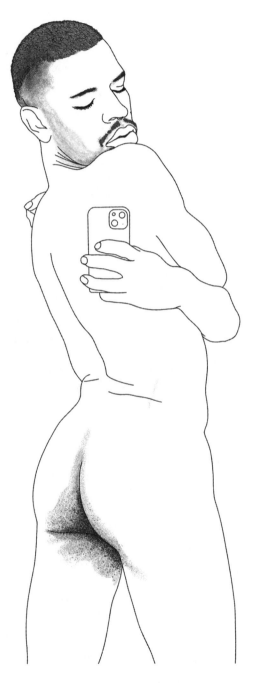

Esther Renehan 🔲 *@clouds.and.cakes.art*

greets. I was like, 'Wow, this is going to be my future. I'm going to be fucking fans who will tell me to my face that they are rooting for the person who he doesn't know caused me the most fucking trouble that whole season.'"

But in the madness, along came Doug. "I meet Doug on Grinder in this newfound sexual liberation of mine where I'm like, 'I'm on Grindr and I am hot.' Trolling late one night, Doug sends me a message saying something corny but really sweet and kind. And because I was so deep in the well of people sending their assholes, or cum shots, or 'party and play?' messages, I was caught off guard by somebody being charming at two in the morning. We started talking; and I think we talked for three or four hours on Grindr just joking and having really good conversations. The kind of interaction that's rare on such a platform."

Enter Doug, the man who would become Yvie's husband: "I grew up in New Hampshire. Right out of high school I moved to Boston for a couple of years. I was there doing community college and working at a restaurant. Then I joined AmeriCorps, which is a domestic version of the Peace Corps. That is what originally took me out to Denver. I must have been twenty-one or twenty-two. For a year I traveled around the Southwest working with non-profits. And I told myself if I liked Denver, I'd move there. I was stationed in Denver and I would go out on all these projects. After that ended, I stayed in Denver. I finished my undergrad in Denver, at the University of Colorado, while working at a restaurant. I was never a traditional student, I was always doing part-time, or almost full-time work. I was there for about five years. But I didn't meet

Yvie until my last year in Denver, actually, right before I was going to leave to go to law school. It was right before the show aired, and I was leaving in September to go to law school. And then I went to law school, and we stayed together. And then the pandemic hit, so I went back to Denver, and we lived together for a year and a half. Then I went back to Boston for school, and now I'm in New York."

How sweet. But where's the dirt? Where's the drama? Where's the tea? Where's the "truth" of the relationship that you hide from other people? "It's funny," Doug says, "because ever since we met, we were very no-drama. Everything just goes great, after the first four or five months, because when I first started talking to them, I was still in a relationship. The part where it gets even messier is that I was in a relationship with a drag queen in Denver." There it is. There's the drama. That's what daddy was looking for.

"I had been dating this guy for two years and it had gotten pretty rocky. I kind of knew that it was nearing its end. But we lived together, which made it . . . It's always hard to break up when you're still living together, and you have expensive rent and everything. It was the night that we [Doug and Yvie] started talking—it was our Grindr-versary, which is what we call it—February 24. That same night I had gone out with friends, and my boyfriend at the time did something to really piss me off. And I just remember that night being like, 'This is over. I'm going to end it within the next couple of days. It's over.' And we were in an open relationship anyway. So, I go home and it's two or three in the morning and I just go on Grindr. I was just bored, in bed, and I saw Yvie on there, but at the time I didn't know it was Yvie. I knew who Yvie was because by then they were kind of big in Denver. And the cast had been announced too, but it hadn't premiered, and so I didn't actually know what they looked like out of drag. And I was also drunk. I messaged them, and I said something like, 'When you want to send nudes, but you're trying to be respectful.' Or something like that. And then Yvie said something like, 'There's no respect in the Grindr world.' And I was like, 'You're right. But I just want to say you're beautiful, blah blah blah.' And we just started talking. And we took it off Grindr within a couple of hours, and then we were up until seven or eight o'clock in the morning just texting. No nudes being shared. It was just electric from the start. But I was still dating this guy, too."

Yvie was taken aback by this situation. What was supposed to be a "wham, bam, thank you Sam" turned into something more. Yvie explains, "He was such an interesting person, especially because he was not at all my type of guy. He's shorter than me, he didn't seem very gay, very queer. He had straight guy friends. He told me that he watched football. It was sounding a little like my ex Andrew. But the difference was, with Doug, from day one, I didn't have to be fake about anything. It was really fun, and we got off on the fact that we disagree on so many things, and that we come from two different walks of life, and that we have two different ways of seeing and walking through the world. Through Doug, I learned that for me to be happy in a relationship I need somebody I can argue with, because I'm going to be a petulant fuck. And not even real arguing, like annoying couples bickering. I just need somebody who will let me be a cantankerous little brat. Like when Doug asks what I want for dinner, and I'm like, 'food.'"

Doug and Yvie had their first date on February 27, 2019—the day before season 11 of *Drag Race* aired. Doug shares, "I just remember being like, 'Oh, tomorrow is your last day of anonymity. How do you feel?' We went out to a bar in Denver, and we were there until closing. They were putting up all the chairs around us and everything. I drove him home, and I was sick with a cold or something. And I was like, 'I really want to kiss you but I'm sick.' And he was like, 'I don't care.' And we kissed, but then I dropped him off and he went home. Which I don't think is like either of us at all. We are not prudes. So, it was kind of funny for the beginning to be very, very coy. And then even on our second date, he had me over and made dinner. It was the cutest little pasta dish, and we watched a movie. He paid his roommates to go to the movies and not be around because he thought that they would be too much for me. But then it was still very messy because I hadn't broken up with my boyfriend yet.

"I can't remember exactly when, maybe after a couple of weeks of talking with Yvie, I broke up with my boyfriend. We lived in a studio apartment, so that part was a little rough. But then it got worse. We were cordial with each other but I didn't tell him that I was dating Yvie. That was too weird because he was a drag queen in Denver. So, he would come home and be like, 'Oh, did you see how Yvie did on *Drag Race*?' And I'd be like, 'Oh, I haven't really seen yet. How did they do?' Our one rule was you don't bring people back to the apartment. And one night I went out and got very drunk and brought not one, but two people back, and they both fell asleep there. My ex-boyfriend came home at three in the morning, went through my phone, and found out I was dating Yvie.

"Then—and this is the most unhinged part—he took pictures of me in bed, asleep with these two guys, and sent them to Yvie. And in the morning, I woke up to it, and thought, 'Oh my God.' He was trying to make me look terrible to Yvie. But it kind of backfired because I immediately went over to Yvie's house, and we had a really beautiful come-to-Jesus moment of how much we meant to each other that early on. And yeah, me and Yvie have never been in a closed relationship, so that wasn't a big deal. It was just so dramatic, and my ex was just so over the top." There is no flavor of drama more intense than gay drama. We didn't invent it. We perfected it.

Beyond the Kardashian-level drama of the ex-boyfriend, Doug and Yvie both describe their relationship as open and honest, and drama-free, but one of the reasons for that may have been that they started dating when Yvie's life was on display for the world to see. Yvie explains how things evolved once episodes of *Drag Race* started to air. "It was nerve-wracking for me—and maybe this is also where the ease and honesty in our relationship came in—because when you're newly dating somebody you only reveal certain parts of yourself to them. Some people can be like, 'I'm completely honest from the start.' No, you are not. You don't take a shit in front of the person that you're trying to fuck for the first time, okay? Nobody's one hundred percent open with who they are in the beginning of a new relationship. And I was only talking to or dating Doug for a week or two before my narrative on the show started to play out. How he would perceive me, not only as a new partner but also a reality television character, with that reflecting on me, was all out of my hands. So, I was fucking nervous.

"In the beginning, while we were still getting to know each other, I wasn't trying to involve him at all. He didn't know anything about where and what I did on the season. He didn't get any info on what was happening. He just got random moments of me crying and being like, 'This is so hard being judged.' And breaking down, but not even being able to tell him why, just being like, 'This is the best I did. This is just going to be such a hard season.' It was amazingly unique because as much support as I had from everyone else in my life, they also knew me before, so there was no pressure for them to see me yelling at bitches, and being kind of petulant, because they already had seen those parts of me and knew to expect it. But the fact that Doug still loved me when he saw that, is a tribute to who he is. He wasn't always on my side. Sometimes he was like, 'Yeah, you came off pretty bad this episode, and you probably shouldn't say anything about it online.' But he was always there. He was always honest and there to broaden my horizons, to open my perspective no matter how much tunnel vision I had."

In the beginning, Doug got to see two versions of Yvie. As he explains, "Yvie on our dates, in person, was so sweet, and funny, playful, and goofy. And then I would watch them on TV, and I'd be like, 'Why are you so angry? You're yelling at everybody. You seem so stressed on that show, and you're so on edge.' I think in the first season the audience really missed how goofy and playful they are. That's why it was weird for me to be watching it because I'm like, 'Man, I cannot picture you getting angry like that.' The other thing is, it was filmed the year before, so the whole timing thing was different too. But it was definitely a trip." That is important context, as the experience of *Drag Race* impacted Yvie significantly and helped them evolve. Who Yvie was when they started filming season 11 wasn't the same person Doug started dating, but Doug and the world got a look at an old version of Yvie, without considering that context. Who we are is not set in stone. Yvie has and will continue to evolve and change.

At first, Doug kept their relationship a secret. "I wasn't telling anyone at first, even some of my closest friends. I don't know why, but I didn't know where it was going to go. I had thought that it was going to be a summer fling because I was leaving to go to law school. It was just a little weird at first. It took a little bit to get used to dating a person in the public eye, but one of the things we always say is that when we met was kind of the perfect timing. Because if I had met Yvie after the show, I would have had so many preconceived notions. I would have felt like I already had an idea of who they were. And if we were dating before they went on the show, I would have had to have gotten used to a completely different lifestyle. So, we always say we got the sweet spot where I didn't have any preconceived notions, but I also wasn't used to a life before *Drag Race*."

Chaos is probably the best word to describe what it's like to date a celebrity. And that chaos can have a serious impact on a relationship. In Doug and Yvie's case, things had their own speed. Yvie shares, "I feel like because our relationship had to start out in such a strange way, in such a strange place, that it was constantly adapting and evolving so much more than I think most people's relationships are in the first year that they're getting to know each other. The first month that we were dating, we were actually in person getting to see each other, like new people would. And then I started traveling, and I was gone for weekends. And that connection became more important because in the middle of the season, it was really hard. And getting all the fan hate, and the bullshit, and the love, and being idolized, and feeling like a sellout, and dealing with fame, and dealing with your friends and family starting to treat you differently. And the only thing I had was Doug, and I realized I was so deeply, madly in love with him. I was very vulnerable going through this experience, and he just held me the whole time, whether it was in person or on the phone. He dated me when I had to shave off my eyebrows because I was working so much. He got to see me in full drag queen mode. I was sacrificing my humanity to be a drag queen. And he still would cum at my nudes." Wow, that is love.

"And the hardest thing for me was, much like my first boy-friend, I knew when I started dating Doug that there would be this point six months down the line where he would leave to go to school across the country and we would become long-distance. But that just happened to line up with my first time going on an international tour and being away for multiple weeks at a time, in what was about to be a string of tours, so I was going to be

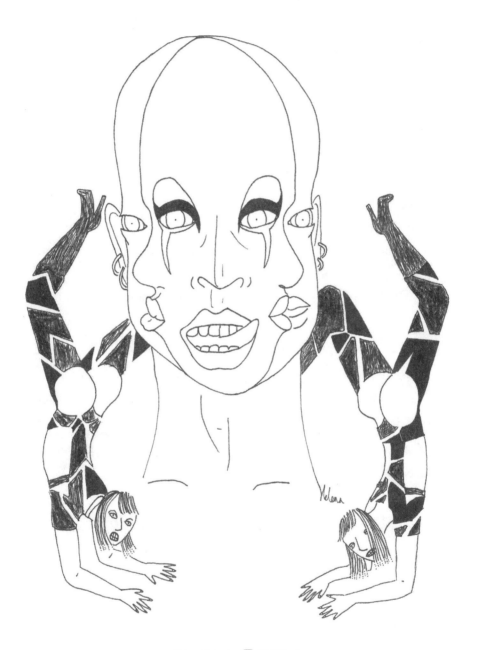

Helena Cabrales 🄾 *@l_h3len4*

gone for two months. And when I got back, the one thing that brought me comfort through all the bullshit was going to be on the other side of the country. So, it was this big scary moment, because part of me was wondering if we were going to break up before then.

"But it was also strange trying to figure out whether or not we were going to be real about this, because we were open the whole time. And the whole time I'm like, 'I'm going to take advantage of the fact that people want to fuck me because I'm famous. And you can take advantage of the fact that I have a great dick and go out there and spread it.' But I didn't want to be fucking other people if I couldn't go home and fuck Doug. So, we stayed together, and we dealt with being apart for two months, which was one of our longest periods. And ever since then we've just been getting to know each other."

Yvie's (self-professed) poor communication skills are not as simple as leaving a text on read. It goes much further. Like when Yvie referred to Doug as their boyfriend during a conversation with their mother but hadn't actually talked with Doug about giving that label to the relationship. Or when Doug was moving back to Boston and he told Yvie that he wanted them to stay together and be in a long-distance relationship, and Yvie had already assumed that was what was happening. That's just who Yvie is. It doesn't mean Yvie isn't deeply committed to the relationship, or questioning things. It's just part of the Yvie experience.

Regardless, it's safe to say that Yvie and Doug are deeply in love, and that was on display in what can only be described as a scene from a Julia Roberts rom-com. Yvie was leaving for Germany, and by the time they got back to Denver, Doug would have moved to Boston. As Doug explains, "We had the most emotional night, where we didn't sleep, we just cried and held each other. And then I dropped them off at the airport, and I wanted to listen to Adele on the way home. But then I remembered as I'm driving away that they left their phone in my car. I had to pull over at the airport, which they don't allow you to do. So, I'm running through the airport with the phone, yelling, 'You fucking idiot.' I gave them the phone, we had one more kiss, and I ran back to the car, where the cops were yelling at me to move. I'm bawling my eyes out and I'm yelling back, 'I fucking know. You do not know the day I've had.'" You can't make this stuff up.

Then, something happened that became a blessing in disguise, at least for Doug and Yvie: COVID-19. The pandemic hit, *RuPaul's Drag Race Live* in Las Vegas shut down, and Doug's school in Boston moved everything to virtual classes. So, after a month in Las Vegas together, Doug and Yvie both went back to Denver. They moved back in with Teena, Morgan, and their respective others, but after a few months of six people and one bathroom, Doug and Yvie got their own apartment.

Doug remembers it similarly. "I was there up until August of 2021. So, I was there for over a year. And it was awesome because one of the questions that you have when you're in a long-distance relationship is, 'How is this going to work when we're together all the time?' And we were together all the time, literally never leaving the house. I was doing all my school in the other room, and it was great. We loved it. We had this little thing where we'd call each other the Sultan of Soup, and we would each make a different soup every week, and that was one of our cute little things. I don't know, I love living with them. I miss them when they go out the door. So it's funny that we're long-distance, when we can also make it work in a pandemic, not leaving a thousand square feet for a couple weeks." The theme of soup returns.

Sadly, for Doug and Yvie (but not the rest of us), pandemic restrictions started to lift. After a little over a year of cohabitation, Doug headed back to Boston, and Yvie returned to Las Vegas. But, as Yvie describes it, that year together made being apart much easier. "I think there's going to be some aspect of me that always wants what I can't have. Because when we were together it was so happy, and so peaceful, and so comforting. He's my best friend, so we just got to be best friends all day, every day. But also, by the end of it I was like, 'I really want to fuck other people, and have adventures, and get lost. And I want to miss you. I see you every day.' So, I think, in my ideal world, our relationship will be where we still live together, but hopefully I'm still busy doing what I'm doing. And he's rich and successful enough to both be flying around the world fucking different boys in every city, and then coming back home to each other and being like, 'Oh baby, I missed you so much. Let's cuddle with our cats.'"

For the most part, Yvie and Doug are living happily ever after. Doug is still in New York, and Yvie is still traveling the world being a famous drag superstar. In July of 2023 they got married, and they bought a place in New York so they can be biresidential, splitting their time between the Big Apple (New York) and the Mile High City (Denver).

Their relationship may not be "traditional," but there will always be an aspect that is unique from that of most other couples: fame. As Doug explains, "It definitely takes a toll, but when it comes to the actual fame part, it's kind of interesting when I see fan interactions. There are such big differences in fan interactions. Some of them can make me feel gross. Some people will come up and they'll say, 'Are you a famous drag queen?' And Yvie will say something snarky, and then they'll be like, 'Okay, let's take a picture.' And it feels so weird because they don't even know Yvie's name, but they just know that they're famous. Then other times I've seen interactions that make me want to cry, where someone will come up to them and be like, 'You mean so much to me,' and then they'll share a moment, and they'll hug. And then sometimes they don't even ask for a picture, they'll just walk away. With those interactions, I'm thinking, 'Yeah, interrupt my dinner for those, that is great.' So, I think with being seen in public, it's really a matter of how the people are, how they act. Because you can act like a fool, or you can act sincere, and it can make all the difference in how it is.

"It's good that I am not a drag queen or an artist in that way, because I think if I was, there would be a lot of jealousy. Part of keeping our lives separate is because I do not want to be famous. I would never want to be famous. I'm not trying to do what they're doing, so I don't feel jealous in that way. I'm amazed at the people all over the world that Yvie touches. I remember once

I showed them this graffiti that someone did in Argentina, and it was a mural of Yvie. And I said, 'Do you realize how fucking cool that is? Do you know how fucking amazing that is? This is incredible. You better never forget how incredible it is, and how incredible you are.'"

Now that is love.

YVIE'S TOP 5 *DRAG RACE* LEWKS THAT WERE SO BAD THEY WERE GOOD

1. LaLa Ri's Bag Ball "The Bag Ball"

2. Kelly Mantle's "RuPaul's Big Opening #1"

3. Serena ChaCha's Garbage Couture "RuPaullywood or Bust"

4. Kennedy Davenport's Death Becomes Her "Ru Hollywood Stories"

5. Jiggly Caliente's Apocalypse Couture "RuPaulcolypse Now"

CHAPTER 11

BACK TO THE FUTURE: WHAT'S NEXT FOR YVIE ODDLY

S
o, what's next for Yvie? That's a great question, and not an easy one to answer. It's not like they're at the end of their career, let alone the middle—they're barely scratching the surface of thirty. It's fair to say that Yvie's journey is far from over. This book isn't a final chapter but a summary of the events that have unfolded so far. The Chronicles of Yvie. And there are many more chapters to come.

When Yvie reflects on where they are today, compared to the person they were when they were desperate to get on *Drag Race*, the word that comes to them is *fine*. "I know that sounds disappointing, but I had so much hunger, and so much passion. And I felt like it was so important to be perceived in a certain way. And I finally feel fine with myself. I've worked on projects that tens of thousands to millions of people give a shit about, and I've done things that I've been really passionate about. I'll get a random occasional fan saying, 'Oh, I like that.' I feel okay with myself. I feel like I'm worth it. Not even 'you deserve to win' kind of worth it, because that's so far in the past for me now. I just feel okay with who I am and how life unfolds for me, positive and negative. I feel fine.

"I think my art is expressing that, because instead of screaming so desperately for somebody to see me, my art is a conversation now. I still want more. I'm still hungry for more. I'm still chasing things. I'm still trying things. So, I feel okay with myself, because even if I don't achieve those things, at least I've gotten to do them. At least I've gotten to try. At least I got to pour some energy into it.

"I feel like I've grown into the crown that was placed on my head years ago. The person that they crowned is really here now. I feel I've started to feel like a legacy. I'm a living legacy. I've seen my impact on the world, and not just because I was on people's televisions. I just feel like a queen, and queens don't have to scream for respect or attention. You just do your best for the people, and you look really good."

Yvie's life is now filled with creative outlets. They continue to perform on tours like Werq the World, as well as their own one-woman show, Strange Love. They find inspiration in the strangest of places. "Inspiration is all over the place. I think the best way

I can summarize the things that inspire me are just things that make me feel: things that scare me, that make me laugh, that make me cry, ideas that stick with me like that. It's half of being a drag queen. Colors, shapes, nature, space. I don't give a shit about people. And it's not like I don't love people, because I love so many people, but that's not what inspires me. I don't care about the pop star, I don't care about the movie trend, I don't care about the meme. I think the only way that people are fun for me, creatively, is to dissect us and make fun of us because we're such fucking ridiculous creatures."

Music has been a big part of Yvie's life and expression. They've released a couple of EPs, receiving very positive reviews. Yvie's music is as unique as they are. It's rap with a pop vibe, but it really defies labels. In an article titled "Yvie Oddly's Debut Album 'Drag Trap' Tells 'Rollercoaster' of Life," *Out* magazine called their first album "expansive, creative, uplifting, and devastating all at once. Moving from the dream-like sounds of tracks like 'Watermelon Bubblegum,' to flows and punchlines that would make veteran rappers sweat, to what surely would've been the club song of the year, the winner of *RuPaul's Drag Race* season 11 is making a big statement with her first album. And that statement says, 'don't underestimate me, bitch.'"

Yvie sees music and rapping as a part of their future, but their perspective has changed. "I've had to completely readjust my views on rapping, because when I first started writing these songs and deciding that I was going to make music, I was partially doing it because I really wanted to see queerness in the rap community, in the mainstream. And we have plenty now, but it's taken away the selfless motivation. Honestly, I like creating it more than I like performing it. It's strange. I like the conceptual, I like piecing the words together, I like rapping them into the microphone, I like shooting the music videos. Still, trying to take that energy seriously on stage is so hard for me. And now I no longer have a desire to be big. I just want to keep working with different artists and keep making music because I like it. It's fun, and I like the process."

Looking toward the future, Yvie has many aspirations. "I want to get back to the root of everything, even before drag, that I have ever wanted to do. And now doing it with this realization that it's not going to—this sounds negative—but it's not going to change my life. Anything I do could change my life, but I'm not looking for something to complete me anymore, which has allowed me a lot more joy in putting things together. I want to do everything I've ever wanted to do. I want to be an artist, I want to be a dancer, I want to be a comic and a singer, I want to have a podcast. I want to be a reclusive Playboy billionaire. Well, a multihundred thousandaire will work. I want to be sexy and dumb. I want to do film, and television and stage productions. I'd love to do interviews and write books. I think this world is absolutely terrible, and I have absolutely no hope for the future as a concept. Which makes me just want to do whatever I want to do right now, whatever sounds good right now.

"I think we all still have dreams of doing bigger and better. I still want to work with more people who are bigger names in the industry because some shallow part of me wants to be like, 'Wow.

Kelly Heuss @UniquelyInvitingDesigns

So, this is what it's like to experience a little bit of your life.' But I think what's changed for me is I'm not seeking to be 'the best' anymore. I'm not seeking to be the biggest anymore. I think my worst nightmare would be becoming straight amounts of famous. I have probably a few million people around the planet who know my name, or who have ever known my name, and that's terrifying. But to have that be a billion sounds so fucking scary. Also, I don't want that sort of financial responsibility and guilt. When I say I'm good, I'm fine. I think I have five years planned ahead that will set me up so I can be happy for the rest of my life. And if things change, that's cool. But I just want to experience it. I want to be seen as a stand-alone individual who doesn't need to do club gigs to pay their rent. But there's a way to do that without putting so much pressure on myself."

A reality Yvie has to face is their health. Yvie isn't like your average queen who may get achy as they get older. Botox and fillers won't address what they're facing. hEDS continues to take a toll on their body and has started to limit some of the things they are able to do. But in true Yvie fashion, they're rolling with the punches and looking at different ways to continue being creative, while living with the reality of hEDS. "I want to kind of transition away from doing all the acrobatic things with my body. And I'm trying to push into that world and explore what other aspects of drag I can bring. I really like comedy, I like podcasts, I like talking to people. So, that's something I've seen myself pursuing more of."

One thing that is undeniable is the impact that Yvie has had on people's lives. There are so many examples of the influence

Yvie has had on the drag world, and on the fans. As Asia O'Hara shares, "My mom used to always say, 'You won't remember what somebody said, but you'll remember how they made you feel.' And that is definitely very true of my friendship with Yvie. First, I remember when they were getting ready for the winners' season of *All Stars*, and they called to ask me a question about some feathers. And I remember that was the first time hearing nerves and concern in their voice. I remember getting off the phone and feeling a little bit more in love with them because they were even more real and authentic.

"I also remember being on the Werq the World tour, and we were in Denmark rehearsing. I remember seeing Yvie's number in rehearsal, and having goosebumps. And I remember telling Brandon Voss, 'Okay, they're not doing radio music or pop music, or Beyoncé or Lady Gaga. But this, what Yvie is doing, is by far the most artistic thing that we have in this show, period.' I remember advocating for them, 'This, what Yvie is doing, the thought process, the music at the beginning, the story that it's telling, the fact that it's somewhat vague so it evokes thought. It makes every person in the audience have to put together the connective tissue for themselves because they're not specifically spelling it out.' And I even told Yvie, I was like, 'Your artistic mind never ceases to amaze me.'

"So, there's been a handful of moments like that with Yvie where I have just been blown away with their commitment to what they want to present. And their ability to take everyday ideas and thought processes and put a new spin on them and turn it into art.

And I think I'm even more amazed because I see a lot of times that people don't get it. And to me, that makes it even more incredible."

Where Yvie goes from here is yet to be seen. But as this chapter of "The Chronicles of Yvie" comes to an end, there is one question that remains unanswered: Where does Jovan end and Yvie begin? That may be a strange question to ask, but Yvie's answer was true to Yvie. It was complex and cerebral. "I think in general, drag is the exploitation of how we want to be perceived, how we want to feel. So, to some extent there is a separation because that is Yvie's number one goal, to just feel what I want to feel, make sure we're having a good time. Just be here, say what I want to say. And that's not always with me in every single aspect of everyday life. When I walk past the crackheads at my front door, I keep my head down and I don't say a fucking word. So, Yvie's not with me there, but there's really not that much of a difference between them. Yvie is just the fun, colorful expression of me. Yvie is the language I was able to use to get all of the ideas of Jovan out there. I've always been goofy, I've been smart, I've been creative, I've been extraordinary, I've been subtle and emotional. There's a lot to me, and there's a lot to all of us. But Yvie is just the name that puts that all to power. Jovan, to me, just means that you know where Yvie came from, which is why I don't really go by Jovan for anybody who's not my family. Because if you know me, you know me as what I built myself into. And it's kind of a privilege to get to claim that you built yourself. That's what Jovan is for."

There's something else different about Yvie today, and that is a level of confidence. It's not that they've sent their inner saboteur packing, but they've read them for filth and put them in their place, at least for now. "I feel more like Brooke Lynn Hytes now than I ever, ever would have imagined in my life. I feel the kind of energy that I felt when I was competing against Brooke. It's a quiet confidence. A sense of calm. But this confidence is deadly because I can do things, and it's not even out of a need to prove anything. And that's also probably why I don't see myself ever doing another, at least drag-related, reality competition. If they want to stick me on an island or something, I'll do a face for them. But I don't want my art to be a competition anymore, because it's not. I'm fine, I'm good."

ACKNOWLEDGMENTS

FROM YVIE

I have to offer unimaginable gratitude to my family for loving me (nearly) unconditionally from day one. Thanks for providing me with the building blocks for a truly beautiful and infinitely rich life of wonderment. I'm in awe of how strong you were to nurture this curious, peculiar spirit in the face of a harsh world in love with uniformity. In case I don't express this as often as I should: I love you so much.

To my sweetest lover baby angel darling, for whom my light shines, thank you for the best years of my life. Every day we spend together you reveal to me the preciousness of living in love. So thank you for giving me the deepest love I've ever known ;) It's the gift I can't help but shamelessly regift to you.

Ummm . . . also, special thanks to everyone I've ever fucked (even if it was bad). Thanks again.

To my teachers, my tribe, to the weirdos, the queers, to human beings: you're so magical. To every single one of my friends that is or ever was, thank you for being a beacon of kindness and kinship in the ΧΑΟΣ. I love you.

I want to give major thanks to Michael Bach, to whom I clearly owe this entire book. Thank you for being so curious about the person underneath the character, and for doing the tireless work to tell that story with as much sincerity as humanity. Thank you for letting me be who I am, and for being patient with how much I hate doing homework. I love you.

But most of all I'd like to thank all my foes. Thank you for the peculiar challenges you pose, which feed the fires of my internal existential furnace. I owe so much of my growth to our relationships, so fuck you . . . and thank you.

FROM MICHAEL

I want to thank everyone who gave their time to create the content of this book: Yvie's parents Jessyca and Sheps; Yvie's husband Doug; Yvie's best friend Teena; Yvie's teacher Deb; and Yvie's fellow Ru girls Asia O'Hara, Brooke Lynn Hytes, Naomi Smalls, Nina Flowers, Silky Nutmeg Ganache, and Venus D-Lite. You were all so generous with your time, and because of you, this book is better than I possibly could have imagined.

I want to thank the entire team at Greenleaf for their support and encouragement. I'm blessed to have an amazing team who helped make this book a reality. Also the team at Voss Events, particularly Brandon and Cherie, for having faith in me and not thinking I was a stalker.

I want to thank my family, who always provide me with all the love and support I need: my father, my sister, my niece, and my husband. And my chosen family, who make my life better by just being my friend: Zach and Tofer, Mike and Shana, and the countless other people who I'm fortunate to know. My mother passed away while I was writing this book, so she wasn't able to read it, but she was my biggest fan and I know she would have loved it.

Lastly, I want to thank Yvie, first for trusting me to help tell their story, and for being as open and honest in the interview process as they were. I started this process as an Yvie Oddly fan, but after dozens of hours of interviews and research, I came to be an Yvie Oddly friend, and I am honored to have you in my life.

ABOUT THE AUTHORS

YVIE ODDLY is an internationally acclaimed drag superstar from Denver, Colorado. Yvie captured the attention of the world when they won the eleventh season of *RuPaul's Drag Race*. *New York* magazine named Yvie one of the most powerful drag queens in 2019 because of their ability to push the boundaries of drag performance art. Since then, they've been polishing their skills as a designer, fine artist, rapper, and comedian, performing to audiences worldwide.

By day, **MICHAEL BACH** is a speaker and thought leader in the field of inclusion, diversity, equity, and accessibility. He is the author of two best-selling and award-winning books: *Birds of All Feathers: Doing Diversity and Inclusion Right* and *Alphabet Soup: The Essential Guide to LGBTQ2+ Inclusion at Work*. By night, he's an obsessed *Drag Race* superfan. He and his husband live in Palm Springs, California, with their two dogs, Sasha and Pepper.